2nd Edition

Ventures

STUDENT'S BOOK

TRANSITIONS

Gretchen Bitterlin • Dennis Johnson • Donna Price • Sylvia Ramirez
K. Lynn Savage (Series Editor)

CAMBRIDGE
UNIVERSITY PRESS

CAMBRIDGE
UNIVERSITY PRESS

University Printing House, Cambridge CB2 8BS, United Kingdom

One Liberty Plaza, 20th Floor, New York, NY 10006, USA

477 Williamstown Road, Port Melbourne, VIC 3207, Australia

314–321, 3rd Floor, Plot 3, Splendor Forum, Jasola District Centre, New Delhi – 110025, India

79 Anson Road, #06–04/06, Singapore 079906

Cambridge University Press is part of the University of Cambridge.

It furthers the University's mission by disseminating knowledge in the pursuit of education, learning and research at the highest international levels of excellence.

www.cambridge.org
Information on this title: www.cambridge.org/9781108449595

First published 2008
Second edition 2014

20 19 18 17 16 15 14 13 12 11 10 9 8 7 6 5 4

Printed in Mexico by Editorial Impresora Apolo, S.A. de C.V.

A catalogue record for this publication is available from the British Library

ISBN 978-1-108-45068-3 Workbook
ISBN 978-1-108-44944-1 Online Workbook
ISBN 978-1-316-98669-1 Teacher's Edition
ISBN 978-1-108-44924-3 Class Audio CDs
ISBN 978-1-108-45050-8 Presentation Plus

Additional resources for this publication at www.cambridge.org/ventures

TO THE TEACHER

What is *Transitions*?

Transitions offers standards-based, integrated-skills material to help prepare adult students for success at work or in an academic setting. Aimed at advanced students, *Transitions* focuses on developing reading and writing skills and features high-interest topics such as building self-confidence, managing interviews, and having a positive attitude.

Unit organization

Within each unit there are five lessons:

LESSON A Get ready The opening lesson focuses students on the topic of the unit. The initial exercise, *Talk about the pictures*, creates student interest and activates students' prior knowledge about the topic. The visuals help the teacher assess what learners already know and serve as a prompt for the key vocabulary of each unit. Next is *Listening*, which is based on a mini-lecture. A note-taking exercise helps students practice listening for main ideas and important details. The lesson concludes with a communicative activity that gives students an opportunity to discuss questions related to the theme.

LESSON B focuses on practical grammar. The lesson moves from a *Grammar focus* that presents the grammar point in chart form; to *Practice* exercises that check comprehension of the grammar point and provide guided practice; and, finally, to *Communicate* exercises that guide learners as they generate original answers and conversations.

LESSONS C and **D Reading** develop reading skills and expand vocabulary. The lesson opens with a *Before you read* exercise, the purpose of which is to activate prior knowledge and encourage learners to make predictions. Next, in *Read*, students read a passage of several paragraphs on a high-interest topic related to the theme of the unit. The reading is followed by *After you read* exercises that check students' understanding and use the reading as a springboard for vocabulary building. The lesson concludes with an activity for practicing summarizing skills.

LESSON E Writing provides writing practice within the context of the unit. This lesson has three sections: *Before you write*, *Write*, and *After you write*. The exercises in *Before you write* provide warm-up activities to activate the language students will need for the writing

task, followed by a writing model and exercises to help students plan the writing they will do in the next section. The *Write* section provides the writing prompt and refers to previous exercises to help guide students' writing. *After you write* provides opportunities for students to check their own work

What components does *Transitions* have?

Student's Book

Each **Student's Book** contains ten topic-focused units. Each unit has five skill-focused lessons. The Class audio and new animated grammar presentations can be accessed via QR codes found on the Student's Book pages.

Workbook

The Workbook is a natural extension of the Student's Book. It has one page of exercises for each lesson in the Student's Book. Workbook exercises can be assigned in class, for homework, or as student support when a class is missed. Students can check their own answers with the answer key in the back of the Workbook. If used in class, the Workbook can extend classroom instructional time by 35 to 40 minutes per lesson.

Teacher's Manual

The Teacher's Manual provides generic lesson-plan guidelines for each lesson in a unit as well as lesson-specific teaching notes. The notes include warm-up activities for the note-taking exercises and suggestions for expanding certain other exercises. Unit, midterm, and final tests, the Student's Book answer key, and the Class audio script for the Lesson A listening exercises are provided at the back of the Teacher's Manual.

Audio files for the reading passages

The Class audio files (including recordings of the readings) can be downloaded at www.cambridge.org/ventures/audio/

The Author Team

Gretchen Bitterlin	Sylvia Ramirez
Dennis Johnson	K. Lynn Savage
Donna Price	

SCOPE AND SEQUENCE

GRAMMAR FOCUS	READING	WRITING
■ Participial adjectives	■ Setting goals for the future ■ Keys for success at work	■ Creating a resume
■ The present passive	■ Understanding self-confidence ■ Building self-confidence	■ Writing a paragraph that identifies a strength and provides supporting examples
■ Indirect (reported) statements	■ Family volunteering ■ Volunteering while at college	■ Clustering ■ Writing a summary paragraph about an article
■ Past perfect	■ Reading about online scams ■ Tips for filling out job applications	■ Writing a cover letter
■ Past modals: *Should(n't) have, could have*	■ Keys for a successful interview ■ Following up after an interview	■ Writing a thank-you note

UNIT TITLE TOPIC	LIST ENING AND SP EAKING	VOCABULARY
Unit 6 **Small talk** pages 52–61 Topic: **Making small talk**	■ Purposes of small talk ■ Appropriate and inappropriate small-talk topics	■ Verb + preposition + *-ing* combinations ■ Phrasal verbs
Unit 7 **Improving relationships** pages 62–71 Topic: **Teamwork**	■ The importance and benefits of teamwork ■ Discussing teamwork ■ Giving advice about problems in the workplace	■ Punctuation, phrases, and clauses to signal definitions ■ Understanding idioms
Unit 8 **Giving and receiving criticism** pages 72–81 Topic: **Types of criticism**	■ Negative and constructive criticism ■ Discussing experiences with criticism ■ Discussing regrets	■ Adverbs ending in *-ly* ■ Defining slang expressions
Unit 9 **The right attitude** pages 82–91 Topic: **Positive and negative attitudes**	■ Behaviors of positive and negative people ■ Discussing positive and negative attitudes	■ Positive and negative words and phrases ■ Suffixes for different parts of speech
Unit 10 **Writing at work and school** pages 92–101 Topic: **Writing**	■ The importance of writing ■ Talking about things people write at work and school	■ Synonyms and antonyms ■ Multiple meanings of words

GRAMMAR FOCUS	READING	WRITING
■ Tag questions	■ Small talk, big problems ■ Strategies for successful small talk	■ Writing a paragraph comparing appropriate and inappropriate topics for small talk
■ The present unreal conditional	■ Bad behavior in the workplace ■ Approaches to dealing with annoying people in the workplace	■ Writing a letter giving advice about a problem at work or at school
■ Past unreal conditional	■ Accepting criticism gracefully ■ The performance evaluation	■ Writing a story about a time when someone criticized you
■ Adverb clauses of concession: *although* and *even though*	■ The power of positive thinking ■ Avoiding a negative attitude	■ Writing a college admissions essay
■ Causative verbs: *make*, have, and *get*	■ E-mail etiquette ■ Good business writing	■ Writing an action plan

CORRELATIONS

UNIT	CASAS	BEST Plus Form A	BEST Form B
Unit 1 **Selling yourself** Pages 2–11	0.1.2, 0.1.5, 0.1.6, 0.2.1, 0.2.4, 2.3.1, 2.3.2, 2.5.5, 2.7.6, 4.1.4, 4.1.7, 4.1.8, 4.1.9, 4.4.1, 4.4.2, 4.6.1, 4.8.1, 4.8.2, 4.8.3, 4.9.1, 6.0.1, 7.1.1, 7.1.4, 7.2.1, 7.2.2, 7.4.1, 7.4.2, 7.4.5, 7.5.1	Overall test preparation is supported, with particular impact on the following items ■ Locator: W1, W2, W3, W4, W5 ■ Level 1: 1.1, 2.1, 2.2, 2.3, 4.2 ■ Level 2: 1.2, 2.1, 3.2, 3.3 ■ Level 3: 1.2, 1.3, 2.1, 2.2, 2.3	Overall test preparation is supported, with particular impact on the following areas: ■ Oral interview ■ Personal information / identification ■ Reading passages ■ Writing notes ■ Time / Numbers ■ Reading signs, ads, and notices ■ Employment / Training
Unit 2 **Building self-confidence** Pages 12–21	0.1.1, 0.1.4, 0.1.6, 0.2.1, 0.2.4, 2.5.1, 2.8.2, 3.1.2, 3.1.3, 3.5.9, 3.6.4, 3.6.5, 4.1.1, 4.1.2, 4.4.1, 4.6.1, 4.8.1, 4.8.5, 4.8.7, 7.1.1, 7.1.4, 8.3.1	Overall test preparation is supported, with particular impact on the following items: ■ W3, W5-6 ■ Level 1: 3.3, 4.2 ■ Level 2: 2.3 ■ Level 3: 4.2	Overall test preparation is supported, with particular impact on the following areas: ■ Oral interview ■ Personal information ■ Communication ■ Directions / Clarification ■ Employment / Training
Unit 3 **Volunteering** Pages 22–31	0.1.1, 0.1.4, 0.1.7, 0.2.1, 1.9.1, 2.2.1, 2.5.1, 2.7.2, 2.7.3, 2.8.3, 2.8.9, 4.3.2, 4.6.1, 4.6.4, 4.8.1, 4.8.2, 7.3.1, 7.3.2, 7.3.3	Overall test preparation is supported, with particular impact on the following items: ■ Level 1: 3.2, 3.3, 4.2 ■ Level 2: 2.2, 2.3 ■ Level 3: 2.2, 4.2	Overall test preparation is supported, with particular impact on the following areas: ■ Oral interview ■ Personal information ■ Communication ■ Directions / Clarification ■ Listening comprehension ■ Reading ■ Writing
Unit 4 **Effective job applications** Pages 32–41	0.1.4, 0.2.1, 0.2.4, 1.9.1, 2.1.1, 2.2.1, 2.3.1, 4.1.1, 4.1.2, 4.1.3, 4.1.4, 4.1.5, 4.1.6, 4.1.7, 4.1.8, 4.2.1, 4.2.3, 4.4.1, 4.4.7	Overall test preparation is supported, with particular impact on the following items: ■ W1, W2, ■ Level 1: 3.2, 4.2 ■ Level 2: 1.2, 1.3, 5.2 ■ Level 3: 3.1	Overall test preparation is supported, with particular impact on the following areas: ■ Reading ■ Writing ■ Fluency ■ Communication ■ Personal information ■ Time / Numbers
Unit 5 **Successful interviews** Pages 42–51	0.1.1, 0.1.2, 0.1.3, 0.1.4, 0.2.1, 0.2.2, 0.2.3, 2.3.1, 4.1.1, 4.1.2, 4.1.5, 4.1.6, 4.1.7, 4.1.8, 4.1.9, 4.2.1, 4.2.5, 4.4.1, 4.4.4, 4.4.5, 4.5.1, 4.5.2, 4.5.4, 4.8.1, 6.0.1, 7.1.3, 7.2.1	Overall test preparation is supported, with particular impact on the following items: ■ W1, W2, ■ Level 1: 3.2, 4.2 ■ Level 2: 1.2, 1.3, 5.2 ■ Level 3: 3.1	Overall test preparation is supported, with particular impact on the following areas: ■ Reading ■ Writing ■ Fluency ■ Communication ■ Personal information ■ Time / Numbers

For more details and correlations to other state standards, go to: www.cambridge.org/ventures/correlations

NRS Educational Functioning Level Descriptors	English Language Proficiency and College and Career Readiness Standards
Interpretive ■ Determine the main topic and key details in a lecture about hard and soft skills. ■ Determine the main idea and key details in a reading about success at work. ■ Determine the meaning of vocabulary based on the context in the reading and the dictionary definition. **Productive** ■ Deliver a short oral presentation about classmates' experiences. ■ Write a summary of a reading about goal setting. ■ Write a resume that includes a career objective, education and job experience, references, and adjectives that describe you as an employee. ■ Report on an Internet research project on interviews with people about their goals. **Interactive** ■ Discuss your desired job and needed hard and soft skills and plan to achieve those skills. ■ Participate in conversations about feelings and opinions. ■ Participate in conversations about your own experiences. ■ Collaborate to develop a summary of a reading about goal setting and a reading about keys for success at work.	ELP Standards 1–10 Reading Anchors 1, 2, 4, 5, 7, 9, 10 Speaking & Listening Anchors 1, 2, 3, 4, 6
Interpretive ■ Determine the main topic of and key details in a spoken text about strengths and weaknesses. ■ Use context clues to determine the meaning of vocabulary about building self-confidence. ■ State an opinion and cite evidence to support it. **Productive** ■ Write a list of your strengths using examples based on personal experiences you have had. ■ Deliver a short oral presentation about a classmate's areas of confidence. ■ Report on a short research project using print and digital sources on self-confidence. ■ Identify and use academic words in a reading about the disadvantage of having too much self-confidence. ■ Write a summary about self-confidence. **Interactive** ■ Participate in conversations about building self-confidence. ■ Discuss with a partner each other's writing about personal strengths. ■ Collaborate to write a summary of a reading about self-confidence.	ELP Standards 1–10 Reading Anchors 1, 2, 3, 4, 5, 6, 7, 9, 10 Speaking & Listening Anchors 1, 2, 3, 4, 6
Interpretive ■ Determine the main topic of and key details in a spoken text about volunteering. ■ Use gerunds to determine the meaning of vocabulary about volunteering. ■ State an opinion and cite evidence to support it. **Productive** ■ Write a one paragraph summary of the article in this unit. ■ Deliver a short oral presentation about a student's volunteer experience. ■ Identify and use academic words in readings about the disadvantages of volunteerism. ■ Write a summary about volunteering at college. **Interactive** ■ Discuss what kind of volunteer work you are interested in. ■ Discuss with a partner each other's writing about the benefits of volunteering in college. ■ Collaborate to write a summary of a reading about volunteering in college.	ELP Standards 1–10 Reading Anchors 1, 2, 4, 5, 7, 9, 10 Speaking & Listening Anchors 1, 2, 3, 4, 6
Interactive ■ Determine the main topic of and key details in a spoken text about applying for a job. ■ Use *suffixes* to determine the meaning of vocabulary about effective job applications. ■ State an opinion and cite evidence to support it. **Productive** ■ Write a cover letter using exercises from this unit. ■ Deliver a short oral presentation about a classmate's important life experiences. ■ Report on a short research project using print and digital sources about the job search process. ■ Write a summary about scammers on the Internet. **Interactive** ■ Discuss your experiences applying for a job. ■ Participate in conversations about effective job applications. ■ Discuss with a partner each other's cover letter. ■ Collaborate to write a summary of a reading about avoiding scammers while applying for jobs online.	ELP Standards 1–10 Reading Anchors 1, 2, 4, 5, 7, 9, 10 Speaking & Listening Anchors 1, 2, 3, 4, 6
Interactive ■ Determine the main topic and key details in a written text about how to have a successful interview. ■ Use context clues to determine the meaning of vocabulary about successful interviews. ■ State an opinion and cite evidence to support it. **Productive** ■ Write a thank-you email using examples from this unit. ■ Deliver a short oral presentation about a classmate's past mistake. ■ Identify and use academic words in a reading about a different way to find "hidden" jobs. ■ Write a summary about the keys to a successful interview. **Interactive** ■ Discuss the five rules for making a good first impression. ■ Participate in conversations about successful interviews. ■ Collaborate to write a summary of a reading about how to have a successful interview.	ELP Standards 1–10 Reading Anchors 1, 2, 4, 5, 7, 9, 10 Speaking & Listening Anchors 1, 2, 3, 4, 6

UNIT	CASAS	BEST Plus Form A	BEST Form B
Unit 6 **Small talk** Pages 52–61	0.1.1, 0.1.2, 0.1.4, 0.1.6, 0.1.8, 0.2.1, 0.2.4, 2.2.1, 2.3.3, 2.6.1, 2.7.1, 2.7.2	Overall test preparation is supported, with particular impact on the following items: ■ W1, W2, W3, W5 ■ W6, W7, W8 ■ Level 1: 1.2, 3.2 ■ Level 2: 1.2, 3.1 ■ Level 3: 1.1, 3.1	Overall test preparation is supported, with particular impact on the following areas: ■ Fluency ■ Communication ■ Personal information
Unit 7 **Improving** **relationships** Pages 62–71	0.1.1, 0.1.2, 0.1.3, 0.1.4, 0.1.6, 0.2.1, 1.2.1, 1.2.6, 1.3.1, 1.4.1, 1.6.1, 2.1.7, 2.2.1, 2.6.3, 2.7.6, 2.7.7, 2.7.8, 2.7.9, 2.8.3, 2.8.4, 2.8.6, 4.2.1, 4.3.2, 4.4.1, 4.4.3, 4.4.4, 4.6.1, 4.6.2, 4.6.4, 4.8.1, 4.8.2, 4.8.5, 4.8.6, 7.3.1, 7.3.2, 7.3.3	Overall test preparation is supported, with particular impact on the following items: ■ W1, W2, W3, W4 ■ Level 1: 2.1, 2.3 ■ Level 2: 2.1, 2.3 ■ Level 3: 1.2, 3.3, 4.1	Overall test preparation is supported, with particular impact on the following areas: ■ Fluency ■ Communication ■ Personal information ■ Directions / Clarification ■ Listening comprehension
Unit 8 **Giving and** **receiving** **criticism** Pages 72–81	0.1.1, 0.1.2, 0.1.3, 0.1.6, 0.1.7, 0.1.8, 4.4.1, 4.4.2, 4.4.4, 4.6.1, 4.8.1, 4.8.2, 4.8.5, 4.8.6	Overall test preparation is supported, with particular impact on the following items: ■ Level 1: 2.3 ■ Level 2: 2.3, 3.2 ■ Level 3: 1.3, 2.1, 2.2	Overall test preparation is supported, with particular impact on the following areas: ■ Fluency ■ Communication ■ Personal information ■ Listening comprehension
Unit 9 **The right** **attitude** Pages 82–91	0.1.1, 0.1.2, 0.1.3, 0.1.6, 0.1.7, 0.1.8, 0.2.1, 4.4.1, 4.4.2, 4.4.4, 4.4.7, 4.6.1, 4.6.5, 4.8.1, 4.8.3, 4.8.5, 4.8.6, 4.8.7	Overall test preparation is supported, with particular impact on the following items: ■ W4, W7, W8 ■ Level 1: 2.2, 2.3, 4.2, 4.3 ■ Level 2: 1.3, 2.1, 2.2, 3.2, 3.3 ■ Level 3: 1.2, 1.3, 2.1, 2.2, 2.3, 3.3, 4.2	Overall test preparation is supported, with particular impact on the following areas: ■ Fluency ■ Communication ■ Personal information ■ Listening comprehension
Unit 10 **Writing at** **work and** **school** Pages 92–101	0.2.2, 0.2.3, 1.7.6, 2.3.4, 2.4.1, 3.2.1, 4.4.7, 4.5.2, 4.5.5, 4.6.2, 4.6.5, 4.7.1, 4.7.4, 5.4.1, 7.1.4, 7.4.2, 7.7.2, 7.7.4	Overall test preparation is supported, with particular impact on the following items: ■ W6, W7, W8 ■ Level 1: 2.3, 4.2, 4.3 ■ Level 2: 2.3, 3.2, 3.3, 4.2 ■ Level 3: 1.2, 1.3, 2.1, 2.2, 2.3, 3.2, 3.3, 4.2, 5.1, 5.2	Overall test preparation is supported, with particular impact on the following areas: ■ Writing notes ■ Reading ■ Writing ■ Fluency ■ Communication

For more details and correlations to other state standards, go to: www.cambridge.org/ventures/correlations

NRS Educational Functioning Level Descriptors

Interactive ■ Determine the main topic of and key details in a spoken text about small talk. ■ Use *prepositions* to determine the meaning of vocabulary about small talk. ■ State an opinion and cite evidence to support it. **Productive** ■ Write a paragraph about appropriate and inappropriate topics for small talk. ■ Role-play small talk with a partner using true and false statements and tag questions. ■ Report on a short research project using interviews about small talk. ■ Identify and use academic words in a reading about making the best of small talk. ■ Write a summary about misunderstandings in small talk. **Interactive** ■ Discuss how to start a conversation with a stranger in different countries. ■ Participate in conversations about small talk. ■ Collaborate to write a summary of a reading about misunderstandings in small talk.	ELP Standards 1–10 Reading Anchors 1, 2, 4, 5, 7, 9, 10 Speaking & Listening Anchors 1, 2, 3, 4,
Interactive ■ Determine the main topic of and key details in a spoken text about the benefits of teamwork. ■ Use *punctuation*, *phrases*, and *clauses* about improving relationships. ■ State an opinion and cite evidence to support it. **Productive** ■ Write a paragraph in which you respond to a letter asking for advice. ■ Deliver a short oral presentation about a classmate's advice for difficult situations. ■ Report on a short research project using print and digital sources about team behaviors. ■ Identify and use academic words in a reading about strategies for dealing with bad behavior. ■ Write a summary about bad behavior in the workplace. **Interactive** ■ Discuss your thoughts and opinions about teamwork. ■ Discuss with a partner each other's writing about improving relationships. ■ Collaborate to write a summary of a reading about bad behavior in the workplace	ELP Standards 1–10 Reading Anchors 1, 2, 4, 5, 7, 9, 10 Speaking & Listening Anchors 1, 2, 3, 4, 6
Interactive ■ Determine the main topic of and key details in a spoken text about giving constructive criticism. ■ Use *adverbs* to determine the meaning of vocabulary about giving and receiving criticism. ■ State an opinion and cite evidence to support it. **Productive** ■ Write a story about a time someone criticised you, and what you learned from the experience. ■ Deliver an oral presentation about something a classmate was sorry that they did or did not do. ■ Report on a short research project using interviews about receiving criticism. ■ Identify and use academic words in a reading about different problems with performance reviews. ■ Write a summary about accepting criticism gracefully. **Interactive** ■ Discuss the three steps of giving constructive criticism. ■ Participate in conversations about giving and receiving criticism. ■ Discuss with a partner each other's writing about receiving criticism. ■ Collaborate to write a summary of a reading about accepting criticism gracefully.	ELP Standards 1–10 Reading Anchors 1, 2, 4, 5, 7, 9, 10 Speaking & Listening Anchors 1, 2, 3, 4, 6
Interactive ■ Determine the main topic of and key details in a spoken text about positive and negative behaviors. ■ Use context clues to determine positive or negative meanings of vocabulary words. ■ State an opinion and cite evidence to support it. **Productive** ■ Write a college admissions essay that responds to the question given in this unit. ■ Deliver a short oral presentation about a classmate's positive and negative thoughts. ■ Report on a research project using print and digital sources about behavior. ■ Identify and use academic words in a reading about problems related to optimism. **Interactive** ■ Discuss some positive and negative people you know. ■ Participate in conversations about having the right attitude. ■ Discuss with a partner each other's writing about having the right attitude. ■ Collaborate to write a summary of a reading about the power of positive thinking.	ELP Standards 1–10 Reading Anchors 1, 2, 4, 5, 7, 9, 10 Speaking & Listening Anchors 1, 2, 3, 4, 6
Interactive ■ Determine the main topic of and key details in a spoken text about the importance of writing. ■ Use *synonyms* and *antonyms* to determine the meaning of vocabulary about writing. ■ State an opinion and cite evidence to support it. **Productive** ■ Write an action plan that includes the problem, consequence(s), recommendation(s), and a timeline. ■ Deliver an oral presentation about things a person made, or convinced another person to do. ■ Report on a short research project using interviews about people's experiences with writing. ■ Identify and use academic words in a reading about the limitations of e-mail. ■ Write a summary about e-mail etiquette. **Interactive** ■ Discuss types of writing you need to do now and how you'd like to improve. ■ Discuss with a partner each other's writing about an action plan. ■ Collaborate to write a summary of a reading about e-mail etiquette.	ELP Standards 1–10 Reading Anchors 1, 2, 4, 5, 7, 9, 10 Speaking & Listening Anchors 1, 2, 3, 4, 6

UNIT 1 SELLING YOURSELF

Lesson A Get ready

1 Talk about the pictures

A What kinds of skills do people need in order to find a good job these days?

B Describe the people in the photos. What skills do you think they have? Do you have these skills?

2 Listening

A Listen and answer the questions.

1. What are two types of job skills?

2. Which type is more important?

◀)) CD1, Track 2

B Listen again. Take notes on the key information.

◀)) CD1, Track 2

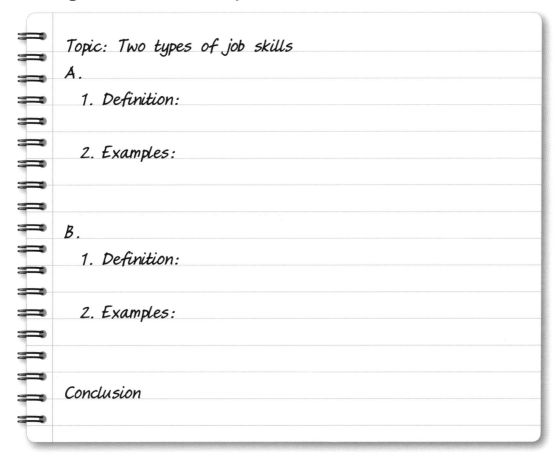

Topic: Two types of job skills

A.

   1. Definition:

   2. Examples:

B.

   1. Definition:

   2. Examples:

Conclusion

Listen again. Check your notes. Did you miss anything important?

C Exchange notes with a partner. Do the notes answer these questions?

1. What are hard skills?

2. What are soft skills?

3. Which type of skill is more important?

D Discuss. Talk with your classmates.

1. What kind of job do you want to have in the future?

2. Which hard and soft skills will you need?

3. What do you plan to do in order to get the skills you need?

Lesson B Participial adjectives

1 Grammar focus: Adjectives ending in *-ed* and *-ing*

Verb forms that end in *-ed* or *-ing* are called *participles*. There is a difference in meaning between the *-ed* and the *-ing* forms. Often, the *-ed* form describes the way someone feels, and the *-ing* form describes a situation, thing, or person.

Adjective *-ed*	Adjective *-ing*	
I'm **interested** in this job.	This is an **interesting** job.	This job is **interesting**.
He's **excited** to do the work.	This is **exciting** work.	The work is **exciting**.

▸ Watch

2 Practice

A Write. Circle the correct adjective.

1. A Josie, how did your job interview at the library go last week?

    B It was really (**tiring**) / **tired**.

2. A Why?

    B It was pretty long. But it was also **excited** / **exciting**.

3. A What did they ask you?

    B They asked if I was **interested** / **interesting** in books.

4. A Did they ask you anything else?

    B They wanted to know if it was **motivated** / **motivating** for me to work on a team or if I preferred working alone.

5. A Do you think you'll get the job?

    B They asked me to come for a second interview tomorrow. I'm so **thrilled** / **thrilling**!

6. A I have an interview at the hospital tomorrow. Do you have any advice for me?

    B Show the employer how **dedicated** / **dedicating** you are.

7. A Anything else?

    B If you don't get the job, don't be **frustrated** / **frustrating**.

8. A Well, I would be **disappointed** / **disappointing**.

    B Just think of it as good interviewing experience.

B **Talk** with a partner. Take turns asking and answering the questions. Choose a participial adjective from the list in your answers.

amazed / amazing   bored / boring   excited / exciting
amused / amusing   disappointed / disappointing   frightened / frightening
annoyed / annoying   embarrassed / embarrassing   surprised / surprising

How do teachers feel when their students are late?

They feel annoyed.

1. How do teachers feel when their students are late?

2. How did Sarah feel when she didn't get her dream job?

3. How does it feel when someone criticizes you in front of other people?

4. What was your opinion about the last movie you saw?

5. What is your opinion about dangerous sports like rock climbing or motorcycle racing?

6. In his job, David sees the same people and does exactly the same things every day. What kind of job does he have?

Write sentences about the situations. Use participial adjectives.

Teachers feel annoyed when their students are late.

3 Communicate

A **Work** in a small group. Take turns asking and answering questions about your experiences. Use the adjectives from Exercise 2B.

What's a frustrating experience you've had at school or work?

I was frustrated when I got a low score on a test after I studied for five hours.

1. What is the most exciting thing that has happened to you recently?

2. Have you ever been depressed?

3. What is an amusing movie or TV show you've seen recently?

4. Is there anything about life in the United States that is surprising for you?

5. [your own question]

B **Share** information with your classmates.

1 Before you read

Talk with your classmates. Answer the questions.

1. What are your goals for the next one, two, or three years?
2. Why are some goals easier than others? Why are some more difficult?

2 Read

Read the article. Listen and read again.

CD1, Track 3

Setting Goals for the Future

What do you want your future to look like? Do you want to develop skills for a better job? Do you want to graduate from college? No matter what you want in the future, one of the best ways to get there is by setting goals.

Setting a goal means making a decision about what you want to achieve. It requires finding out what you need to do to achieve that goal and planning how long it will take you to do it.

Making choices about the future can be difficult because we often focus only on the present. In order to think about your future goals, take a few minutes and imagine what you want your life to be like in one, two, or three years. Where will you be? What will you be doing? How will you feel?

There are a number of important points for you to keep in mind when setting a goal. It should be detailed, measurable, and realistic, and it should have a completion date.

Once you have a goal in mind, try to add as much detail as possible. Adding detail will make the goal clearer. For example, instead of saying "I want to get a better job," you can add details, such as "I want to study cooking so that I can be a chef." Details like "study cooking" and "be a chef" clearly show what you want to achieve and how you plan to achieve it.

In addition to adding detail to your goal, make sure you can measure your progress. "I want a better education" is a good goal, but it is difficult to measure. How will you know when your goal is completed? "I will apply to three colleges next spring" is a better goal because you can pay attention to your progress.

Goals should be challenging, but they should not be too difficult. An impossible goal will lead to failure. You can avoid failure by making sure your goal is realistic. Becoming a professional soccer player might be your dream, but is it realistic? Instead, set your goal on something more achievable, like playing for a local team.

Finally, make sure your goal has a completion date, or deadline. If you know when you want to complete your goal, you will be more motivated. Without a deadline, people often stop paying attention to their goal. Just as your goal should be realistic, your deadline should be realistic also.

3 After you read

A **Check** your understanding.

1. What does *setting a goal* mean? _____

    _____

2. The article describes four characteristics of a good goal. What are they? _____

    _____

3. Why should a goal be detailed? _____

    _____

4. Why shouldn't you have a goal that is too difficult? _____

    _____

5. What happens when people have a goal without a deadline? _____

    _____

B **Build** your vocabulary.

1. Underline the words from the chart in the reading. Then use a dictionary and write the correct definition to fit the meaning of the words as they are used in the reading.

Vocabulary	Definition
1. progress (n.)	*movement toward a goal*
2. realistic (adj.)	
3. measure (v.)	
4. challenging (adj.)	
5. achieve (v.)	

2. Use the words in the chart to form sentences about your goals.

C **Summarize** the reading. Work with a partner and take turns restating the main points. Then work together to write a summary. Include the following:

1. definition of setting a goal

2. four characteristics of a good goal

Lesson D Reading

1 Before you read

Talk with your classmates. Answer the questions.

1. What types of skills do employers look for?
2. What types of personal qualities do employers look for?

2 Read

Read the article. Listen and read again.

CD1, Track 4

Keys for Success at Work

Many people think that employers are only interested in technical skills when they interview new candidates for a job; however, in today's job market, most companies are looking for much more. Different companies have different needs, yet there are a number of general skills and qualities they all hope to find. These skills include:

Communication skills – Companies are interested in people who can communicate and get along well with others. The way you organize your thoughts, express your ideas, and deal positively with customers and co-workers is what will impress employers the most.

Leadership skills – Many companies ask for people who are "self-starters" and who are willing to lead others. In other words, employers want people who can think for themselves and who aren't afraid to make independent decisions.

Maturity – A mature employee is someone who manages time well, takes responsibility for mistakes, and does not become frustrated in challenging situations.

Problem-solving skills – Problem-solving and critical-thinking skills are also very important to employers. Companies value employees who are able to recognize problems, develop a plan for solving them, and follow through with that plan.

Commitment – Employers prefer workers who work hard toward the company's goals. They want to hire team players who are committed to their jobs.

Informational skills – Your ability to gather, organize, and analyze information is very important in today's world. Knowing how to use a computer to search the Internet, send emails, and solve problems is key in almost every profession.

As you can see, most of these do not involve technical skills. They are "people skills" that are important in every job or field. If you lack any of these skills or qualities, you should look for ways to develop them as part of your goal setting for the future.

3 After you read

A **Interpret** the article. Work with a partner. Match each skill with the *best* example. Write the letter of the example in the blank.

Skill

_____ 1. communication

_____ 2. leadership

_____ 3. maturity

_____ 4. problem solving

_____ 5. commitment

_____ 6. informational

Example

a. A new worker at an ice cream store forgets to close the freezer and the ice cream melts. He offers to pay for the ice cream and promises to be more careful in the future.

b. A company needs to find ways to save money. A worker thinks of a plan to save money by reducing the amount of paper that the company is wasting.

c. Melinda's company has an important deadline tomorrow. Her co-workers go home at 5:30 p.m., but she works late into the evening to help the company meet its deadline.

d. A customer at a dry cleaning store is upset because the cleaner damaged his suit. The cashier listens politely and offers to pay for the damage. The customer is satisfied.

e. An auto worker knows how to use a complex computer program to analyze the problem with a customer's car.

f. At a factory, the workers complain that the lunchroom is unattractive. A worker organizes and supervises a group of volunteers who come in on the weekend to decorate the lunchroom.

B **Build** your vocabulary. Underline the words or phrases from the chart in the reading. Use a dictionary and write the correct definition to fit the reading. Write one or two related words and their part of speech.

Word in reading	Definition	Related words
1. impress (v.)	*to please somebody deeply*	*impression (n.), impressive (adj.)*
2. get along with (v.)		
3. maturity (n.)		
4. committed (adj.)		
5. value (v.)		
6. analyze (v.)		

C **Summarize** the reading. Work with a partner and take turns restating the main points. Then work together to write a summary. Include the following:

1. communication skills

2. leadership skills

3. maturity

4. problem-solving skills

5. commitment

6. informational skills

For additional development of College and Career Readiness skills, see "Problems with Goal Setting," a related reading and activities on pages 102–104.

Read closely to determine what a text says explicitly and to make logical inferences; use a dictionary to determine the meaning of words and phrases as they are used in a text; summarize a text

Lesson E Writing

1 Before you write

A **Talk** with a partner. Answer the questions.

1. Why are résumés important for a job?

2. Do you have a résumé? Have you ever used a résumé when you looked for a job?

B **Read** the sample résumé.

Renee Smith

200 Chestnut Rd., Atlanta, GA 30341
(404) 555-1111 • jsmith@cup.org

OBJECTIVE
Teacher's Assistant in a preschool. I am organized,
hardworking, and dedicated to working as a team member.
I am very interested in working with children
with disabilities.

EDUCATION
AA, Early Childhood Education
Atlanta Metropolitan College, Atlanta, GA

High School Diploma
International High School, Atlanta, GA

EXPERIENCE
Teacher's Aide
Little Angels Preschool, Athens, GA
June 2017–present

Tutor
Center for Autism, Athens, GA
October 2016–June 2017

REFERENCES
Available on request

C **Work** with a partner. Answer the questions.

1. Whose résumé is this?

2. What job would this person like to have?

3. What adjectives did this person use to describe herself?

4. Where did this person go to college and high school? What degree does she have?

5. What job experience does she have?

6. How can employers get her references?

D **Plan** your résumé. Complete the information.

1. Your name and address: _____

2. Your job objective (the kind of job you'd like to have): _____

3. Adjectives that describe you as a worker: _____

4. Where you went to school: _____

5. Any job experience that you've had: _____

6. Your references: _____

2 Write

Write your résumé. Use the résumé in Exercise 1B and your outline in Exercise 1D to help you. (Note: You do not need to include references in your résumé, but you must have them if an employer asks for them.)

3 After you write

A **Check** your writing.

	Yes	No
1. I included my name, address, phone number, and email.	☐	☐
2. I included my job objective.	☐	☐
3. I included my education and job experience.	☐	☐
4. I included information about my references.	☐	☐
5. I included adjectives that describe me as a worker.	☐	☐

B **Share** your writing with a partner.

1. Exchange résumés with your partner. Read your partner's résumé.

2. Comment on your partner's résumé. Ask your partner a question about the résumé. Tell your partner one thing you learned.

UNIT 2 BUILDING SELF-CONFIDENCE

Lesson A Get ready

1 Talk about the pictures

A How do you define self-confidence?

B Do you think the people in the photos are self-confident? Why or why not?

2 Listening

A **Listen** and answer the questions.

1. What was the listening about?

2. Who is more self-confident, David or Sarah? Why?

 CD1, Track 5

 CD1, Track 5

B **Listen again.** Take notes on the key information.

David

   Strengths:

   Weaknesses:

Sarah

   Strengths:

   Weaknesses:

Listen again. Check your answers. Did you miss anything important?

C **Exchange** notes with a partner. Do the notes answer the following questions?

1. What are David's strengths and weaknesses?

2. What are Sarah's strengths and weaknesses?

D **Discuss.** Talk with your classmates.

1. Do you agree with the decision to promote David? Why or why not?

2. Why do you think self-confident people are more successful?

3. Are you self-confident? Why or why not?

Lesson B The present passive

1 Grammar focus: Subject + *be* + past participle

Passive sentences have the form subject + *be* + past participle. A passive verb is used to focus on what happens to the subject. A phrase consisting of *by* + noun comes after the passive verb only if it is important to know who or what performs the action.

Active	Passive	
Life experiences **affect** self-confidence.	Self-confidence **is affected** by <u>life experiences</u>.	 Watch
<u>The support you receive</u> **determines** your inner feelings.	Your inner feelings **are determined** by <u>the support you receive</u>.	

2 Practice

A Write. Is the sentence active or passive? Write *A* or *P*.

_P_ 1. The employees are encouraged by their supervisor to have a good attitude.

____ 2. Charles is often criticized by his professors for being late.

____ 3. The economy discourages Mr. Chung from leaving his job.

____ 4. Hugo's job performance is improved by being more positive.

____ 5. Sun Mi is motivated by Kevin's hard work.

____ 6. Mr. Chu improves his résumé using the Internet.

____ 7. Carmela criticizes Kevin for being late.

Change the passive sentences to active sentences. Change the active sentences to passive sentences.

8. *The supervisor encourages the employees to have a good attitude.*

9. _____

10. _____

11. _____

12. _____

13. _____

14. _____

B **Talk** with a partner. Read the ad for the self-confidence workshop. Discuss the questions below.

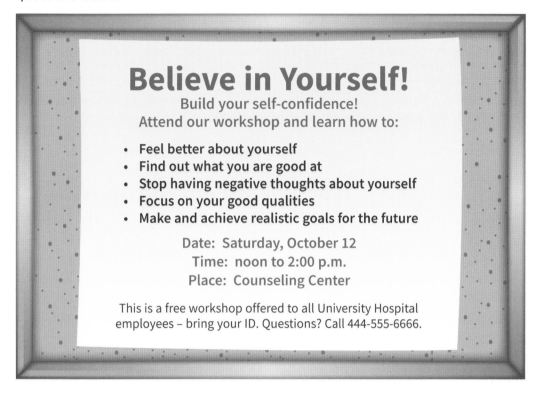

Believe in Yourself!
Build your self-confidence!
Attend our workshop and learn how to:

- Feel better about yourself
- Find out what you are good at
- Stop having negative thoughts about yourself
- Focus on your good qualities
- Make and achieve realistic goals for the future

Date: Saturday, October 12
Time: noon to 2:00 p.m.
Place: Counseling Center

This is a free workshop offered to all University Hospital employees – bring your ID. Questions? Call 444-555-6666.

> What does the workshop encourage you to do?

> You are encouraged to feel better about yourself.

1. What does it discourage you from doing?

2. Where is the workshop located?

3. To whom is the workshop offered?

4. When is the workshop scheduled?

Write answers to the questions. Use the present passive.

3 Communicate

A **Work** with a partner. Talk about self-confidence. Use these phrases to help you:

My self-confidence is affected when . . .

I am encouraged by . . .

When I am criticized by others, I . . .

Sometimes, I am discouraged from . . .

I am motivated to do my best when . . .

My grades are improved when . . .

B **Share** your information with the class.

1 Before you read

Talk with your classmates. Answer the questions.

1. Did you ever feel a lack of self-confidence? What happened?

2. Do your friends or family ever put pressure on you? How?

2 Read

Read the article. Listen and read again.

🔊 CD1, Track 6

Understanding Self-Confidence

What Is Self-Confidence?

Self-confidence means believing in yourself and your abilities. It means being ready and willing to face new situations and accomplish difficult tasks. Self-confident people are usually eager, assertive, motivated, willing to accept criticism, emotionally mature, optimistic, and productive. People who don't have self-confidence lack the inner belief in their ability to be successful. They tend to be withdrawn, unmotivated, overly sensitive to criticism, distrustful, and pessimistic. They don't feel good about themselves. Often they feel like failures.

What Affects Self-Confidence?

Self-confidence is affected by life experiences. You are influenced by parents, siblings, friends, and teachers. From them, you learn how to think about yourself and the world around you. It is the support and encouragement you receive from the people around you – or the lack of it – that helps shape your inner feelings about yourself.

A nurturing environment that provides positive feedback improves self-confidence.

People learn by making mistakes, and they need to feel that missteps along the way are to be expected. However, when friends, family, and others offer unfair criticism, hold unrealistic expectations, or put too much pressure on a person, self-confidence can be affected.

Several different types of behavior show a lack of self-confidence:

1. You judge yourself or your abilities too harshly, or you are overly critical of your performance.

2. You focus too much on your failures and see them as negative events instead of learning experiences.

3. You place too much pressure or stress on yourself to succeed.

4. You set goals that are unrealistic and above your abilities.

5. You are fearful of not succeeding or making mistakes.

A lack of self-confidence can often keep people from achieving their full potential. That's why it's important to get help if you are affected by this problem.

3 After you read

A Check your understanding.

1. People who don't have self-confidence lack some characteristics. What are they?

   _____

2. Name groups of people who influence how you think about yourself.

   _____

3. Name three behaviors that show a lack of self-confidence.

   _____

B Build your vocabulary. Match the words from the reading with their definitions.
Use a dictionary to help you.

__c__ 1. motivated (adj.)

____ 2. criticism (n.)

____ 3. influence (v.)

____ 4. stress (n.)

____ 5. succeed (v.)

a. achieve or complete something good that you have been trying to do

b. try to change the way someone thinks or behaves

c. when someone wants to do something

d. a feeling of tension and worry

e. saying that someone or something is bad

Complete the sentences. Use the correct word from the list above.

6. Steve wants to pass the test, but he is tired and needs help to get _____.

7. John's parents had a lot of _____ on how he thinks about the world.

8. Ms. Chu wants to _____ and works hard to achieve her goals.

9. Lisa puts a lot of pressure on herself and often suffers from _____.

10. Even though Sally is Janet's best friend, Sally often gives her unfair _____.

C Summarize the reading. Work with a partner and take turns restating the main points. Then work together to write a summary. Include the following:

1. definition of self-confidence

2. causes of a lack of self-confidence

3. behavior that shows lack of self-confidence

4. ways to improve self-confidence

Lesson D Reading

1 Before you read

Talk with your classmates. Answer the questions.

1. The article talks about ways to build self-confidence. What are some things you think it will say?

2. Do you think you are self-confident? Why or why not?

2 Read

Read the article. Listen and read again.

Building Self-Confidence

How Do You Build Self-Confidence?

Self-confidence is not built overnight. It is a process that begins by first understanding why you lack confidence, then taking active steps to change your negative thinking and behaviors into positive ones.

First, think about why you lack confidence. Perhaps you are unhappy with your appearance, your social or academic achievements, or the way a relationship ended. Try to identify these feelings and perhaps talk about them with someone you trust. It may surprise you that others share the same kinds of self-doubts or have ones of their own. See your fears as challenges you can overcome – don't let them have power over you!

Steps to Building Self-Confidence

Think of building self-confidence as a process. Aim to make small, positive steps toward success. Practice these strategies until they become your new habits.

1. Think about your good qualities. Are you conscientious, loyal, reliable, and cooperative? Recognize your talents and abilities; these will help you feel better about yourself.

2. Think positively about yourself and what you set out to do. Negative thoughts lead to worry, which can confuse you and keep you from achieving success.

3. Set realistic goals that you can truly reach, both large and small. Praise yourself when you reach even the smallest goals, but keep striving for the bigger ones.

4. Focus on your successes and not on your failures. Realize that everyone makes mistakes, and let yours be tools for learning.

5. Be assertive. It is essential for people to express their thoughts, feelings, and emotions to others. You are entitled to your opinion, and you have important things to say. Don't be afraid to say them.

6. Find a creative outlet for self-expression. Find an activity that lets your abilities shine, such as music, art, cooking, crafts, or sports. You don't have to be the best at what you do, but the risks you take and the things you create provide a fast route to greater self-acceptance.

3 **After you read**

A **Interpret** the article. Work with a partner and take turns reading aloud the six strategies for building self-confidence. Then read the descriptions below, and fill in the blank with the number (or numbers) of the strategies that match each example.

_2_ 1. Jessie is applying to be a manager at work. She knows it will be hard at first, but she is focusing on positive things like the opportunity to learn new skills.

_____ 2. Iris was very busy and forgot to register for the class she wanted. She had to sign up for an evening class instead. She knows other students who made the same mistake. Instead of feeling bad about herself, she plans to register early next semester.

_____ 3. Mr. Morales doesn't like his job, but he loves to play guitar. After work every day Mr. Morales spends an hour practicing guitar. This helps him have a positive attitude about himself.

_____ 4. Ali was shy about sharing his ideas in class. Nevertheless, one day he shared his opinion with his classmates. His thoughts helped create an important discussion.

_____ 5. Mrs. Chang feels good about herself even when she has a setback because she knows she is smart and a very hard worker.

B **Build** your vocabulary.

1. Underline the adjectives from the chart in the reading. Then use a dictionary and write the correct definition to fit the meaning of the word as it's used in the reading.

Vocabulary	Definition
1. conscientious	*showing great care in performing a job or task*
2. reliable	
3. cooperative	
4. assertive	
5. creative	

2. Use the adjectives to write sentences about yourself.

C **Summarize** the reading. Work with a partner and take turns restating the main points. Then work together to write a summary. Include the following:

1. ways to build self-confidence

2. six steps to building self-confidence

For additional development of College and Career Readiness skills, see "Dangers of Too Much Self-Confidence," a related reading and activities on pages 105–07.

Lesson E Writing

1 Before you write

A **Talk** with your classmates. Answer the questions.

1. Why do you think employers or schools want to know about your personal strengths?

2. What are your personal strengths?

B **Read** the personal-strength word list. Put a check mark next to the words you know. Put a question mark next to the ones you don't know.

Personal-strength words

_____ ambitious	_____ enthusiastic	_____ professional
_____ analytical	_____ flexible	_____ reliable
_____ assertive	_____ hardworking	_____ resourceful
_____ attentive	_____ knowledgeable	_____ responsible
_____ cheerful	_____ loyal	_____ a team player
_____ conscientious	_____ motivated	_____ a troubleshooter
_____ dependable	_____ organized	_____ trustworthy
_____ detail-oriented	_____ outgoing	
_____ diplomatic	_____ polite	
_____ energetic	_____ productive	

C **Talk** with a partner. Write a synonym or definition of the words that are new for you. If necessary, use a dictionary.

2 Write

A **Write.** Look again at the list of personal-strength words. Choose two of your best personal strengths from the list and write them down.

Strength #1: _____

Strength #2: _____

B **Write.** Describe your strengths. Write an example of each strength based on an experience you had.

Example:

Strength: I am enthusiastic. At my last job as a busgirl, even though I didn't earn much money, I was always in a good mood and I did my job well. I was motivated to do a good job. Also, I was friendly to the customers and I made them feel comfortable.

Strength #1: _____

_____

_____

_____

_____

Strength #2: _____

_____

_____

_____

_____

3 After you write

A **Check** your writing.

	Yes	No
1. I identified two strengths.	☐	☐
2. I gave an example for each strength.	☐	☐
3. I used active and passive verbs correctly.	☐	☐

B **Share** your writing with a partner.

1. Take turns. Read your writing to a partner.

2. Comment on your partner's writing. Ask your partner questions. Tell your partner one thing you learned.

UNIT 3 VOLUNTEERING

Lesson A Get ready

1 Talk about the pictures

A Why do you think many people choose to volunteer?

B Where are the people in the pictures volunteering? Describe each job. If you could choose one of these volunteer jobs, which one would you choose? Why?

2 Listening

A **Listen** and answer the questions.

1. What was the main idea of the lecture?

2. What are some benefits of volunteering?

3. What are some examples of volunteer opportunities?

CD1, Track 8

B **Listen again.** Take notes on the key information.

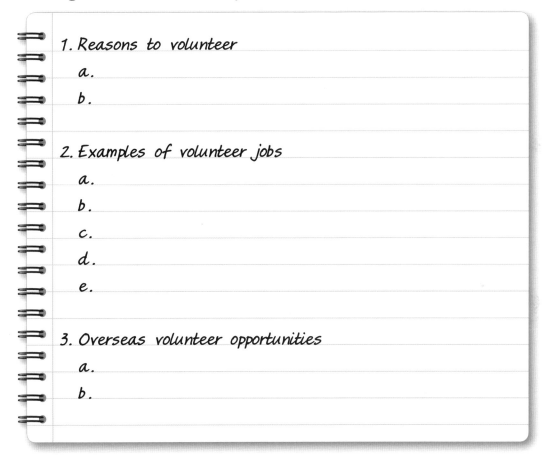

1. Reasons to volunteer

   a.

   b.

2. Examples of volunteer jobs

   a.

   b.

   c.

   d.

   e.

3. Overseas volunteer opportunities

   a.

   b.

CD1, Track 8

Listen again. Check your answers. Did you miss anything important?

C **Exchange** notes with a partner. Do the notes answer the following questions?

1. Why can volunteering be a very beneficial experience?

2. What are some examples of places to volunteer?

3. What are some volunteer jobs that you can do overseas?

D **Discuss.** Talk with your classmates.

1. Are you interested in volunteering? Why or why not?

2. What kind of volunteer work are you good at?

3. How could volunteering help you in the future?

Listen for and identify examples and benefits of volunteering **UNIT 3** 23

Lesson B Indirect (reported) speech

1 Grammar focus: Indirect statements

Indirect, or reported, speech is used to report what someone has said. When changing present statements to past, the verbs in both clauses change to past in formal English. Quotation marks are not used.

Direct statements	Indirect statements
"I volunteer at my local school."	She said (that) she volunteered at her local school.
"I'm enjoying my tutoring job."	She said (that) she was enjoying her tutoring job.
"We can't find jobs," they said.	They said (that) they couldn't find jobs.
"I'm not good at carpentry," said Rebecca.	Rebecca said (that) she wasn't good at carpentry.
"I don't like answering phones," Rob said.	Rob said (that) he didn't like answering phones.

Watch

2 Practice

A **Write.** A volunteer coordinator is talking to a person who is interested in volunteering. Change her statements into indirect speech.

1. "Volunteering is a wonderful way to gain experience for a job."
   She said that volunteering was a wonderful way to gain experience for a job.

2. "We have many different types of volunteer jobs."
   _____

3. "Volunteers can work in a school, hospital, nursing home, or library."
   _____

4. "We don't need volunteers at the animal shelter right now."
   _____

5. "It's a good idea to include volunteer experience on a résumé."
   _____

6. "We're looking for several people to help with beach clean-up this weekend."
   _____

B **Talk** with a partner. Discuss what John said about the volunteer positions in the newspaper.

A What did John say about working in an animal shelter?

B He said that he was not really interested in working with animals.

Volunteer positions	What John said
1. Working in an animal shelter	"I'm not really interested in working with animals."
2. Tutoring elementary school students in an after-school reading program	"I prefer to work with adults."
3. Running errands for elderly home-bound (unable to leave home) people	"I like to help elderly people."
4. Building houses for low-income people	"I'm good at building and carpentry."
5. Removing graffiti from public buildings	"I can do this, but I don't want to do it for long periods of time."
6. Preparing food baskets at the local food bank.	"I live too far from the food bank."

Write sentences about John. Use indirect speech.

John said that he was not really interested in working with animals.

3 **Communicate**

A **Work** with a partner. Role-play conversations between a volunteer coordinator and a university student who is interested in becoming a volunteer.

A What kind of work are you interested in?

B I'm getting my degree in early childhood education, so I want to volunteer with young children.

A We have some volunteer positions working at a day-care center.

B **Perform** your role play for the class.

C **Talk** with your partner. After each role play, report what the counselor and student said. Use indirect speech.

The student said that she was getting her degree in early childhood education and that she wanted to volunteer with young children. The counselor said that they had some volunteer positions working at a day-care center.

Lesson C Reading

1 Before you read

Talk with your classmates. Answer the questions.

1. Have you and your family ever done any volunteer work together?

2. Does your school have a recycling program? Who runs it?

3. Look at the title. What do you think this article is about?

2 Read

Read the article. Listen and read again.

COMMUNITY NEWS

Volunteering
the Family Way

CD1, Track

For sisters Sarah and Audrey Granger of central Missouri, school and volunteering go hand in hand. Community college sophomore Sarah was recently made Student Coordinator for Recycling at her school – a new, paid position for the college. She immediately started to work by developing a central recycling site, ordering new collection bins for campus buildings, and recruiting her younger sister, Audrey, to be her first volunteer.

Audrey, in her first year at the college, wasn't sure she had time for a volunteer job. With all her classes, she said, she thought it would be too much work. "But after working with Sarah and learning how to collect and organize the material for recycling, I discovered it was easier than I thought," she said.

Because of the instant popularity of the recycling project, Audrey said that she quickly understood the value of her volunteer work. "I started to get the idea that you could make a difference and, after a while, reusing and recycling just became part of my lifestyle."

As coordinator of the campus-wide program, Sarah supervises four volunteers, including her sister. The team has worked hard to introduce recycled paper products in the cafeteria and to use plant waste as compost material in the college's gardens. "It's better to reuse some of the food waste from the cafeteria instead of dumping it in the community landfill," Audrey explained.

For Sarah, who is majoring in environmental studies, the position of Student Coordinator is a perfect way to combine her passion for the environment and her interest in volunteering. She said she became interested in volunteering as a child. "My mother works for Habitat for Humanity," she said, "and I used to spend a lot of time helping her with her projects."

In order to keep the recycling program "going and growing," Sarah said people need to use it and support it as much as possible. With committed volunteers like her sister Audrey, there's no doubt that the program has a bright future.

3 **After you read**

A **Check** your understanding.

1. Sarah and Audrey work together at school. How are their duties different?

_____

2. What did Audrey say at first about volunteering?

_____

3. What are two ways recycled products are used at this school?

_____

4. What did Sarah say was necessary for the recycling program to keep "going and growing"?

_____

B **Build** your vocabulary. Prefixes add meaning to words. Find and underline the words in the reading. Circle the prefixes, and then fill in the chart. Use a dictionary if necessary.

Word(s) from reading	Prefix	Meaning of prefix
recycle, reuse	re-	1.
collection	col-	2.
coordinator	co-	3.
supervise	super-	4.
community, combine, committed	com-	5.

Complete the sentences. Write the correct word from the chart.

6. Jorge enjoys working by himself. He does not like to _____ other people.

7. My family likes to _____ Popsicle sticks. We do art projects with them.

8. Mrs. Chavez has a beautiful _____ of glass animals.

9. The students plan to _____ their money and rent a car for a trip to the mountains.

10. James got a new job. He is the new _____ of volunteer projects at the art museum.

C **Summarize** the reading. Work with a partner and take turns restating the main points. Then work together to write a summary. Include the following:

1. Sarah's job
2. Audrey's job
3. How recycled products are used at the school
4. Sarah's hope for the recycling program

Lesson D Reading

1 Before you read

Talk with your classmates. Answer the questions.

1. Do you think it is common for college students to volunteer?

2. Should college students volunteer? Why? Why not?

2 Read

Read the article. Listen and read again.

CD1, Track 10

Volunteering
WHILE AT COLLEGE

IT'S NO SECRET that college students have busy lives. Classes, jobs, and studying often leave very little free time for anything else.

Despite their schedules, however, college students are volunteering more than ever, according to a 2006 study by the Corporation for National and Community Services. In fact, the study said college students are more likely to participate in volunteer activities than other people their age not enrolled in college.

There are many benefits to volunteering while in college. First of all, in many states students can get college credit for helping local organizations. In Massachusetts, for example, many students at Holyoke Community College volunteer at community organizations. In return for their good deeds, the students receive credit and are one step closer to graduating.

In order to volunteer for credit, students need to first talk to their advisor. They often need to provide information about the work and the number of hours it will take. The volunteer work is typically related to the student's major.

A second benefit is that volunteering can help satisfy college requirements. At the University of California, Santa Barbara, honor students must volunteer for at least 20 hours during their last two years on campus. This "community-service requirement" is becoming more and more common in schools across the country.

A third benefit to volunteering involves getting a job. Volunteer work looks great on a graduate's résumé. When an employer sees community service on your résumé, it says you want to help others and are curious about the world around you. These characteristics can help get you an interview.

Whether you volunteer for credit, to meet a requirement, or to improve your résumé, keep in mind the most important aspect of community service: making a difference.

③ After you read

A Check your understanding.

1. Who volunteers more, college students or people of the same age not enrolled in college?

2. What are ways that students benefit from volunteering?

3. A college student wants to volunteer for credit. What should he or she do first?

4. What is a community-service requirement?

5. The article suggests putting volunteer work on your résumé. What are two things that volunteering says about you?

B Build your vocabulary. English has many kinds of nouns. For example, verb + -ing forms, called *gerunds*, often have the meaning of actions or processes. Other nouns refer to people. Look at the gerunds in the chart. Fill in the related nouns that refer to the person who does the action.

Action	Person
volunteering	1.
studying	2. *student*
helping	3.
graduating	4.
participating	5.

Complete the sentences with a noun from the chart.

6. Joseph got three college credits for _____*volunteering*_____ at the local teen center last semester.

7. My guidance counselor is going to be a _____ in a conference on volunteer opportunities in our community.

8. One day a week Mrs. Flowers is a teacher's _____ in her granddaughter's kindergarten class.

9. My parents came to the United States from Romania. They worked hard and sent me to college. I am the first college _____ in the history of my family.

10. My parents don't want me to work while I am in school. "_____ is your job now, and it's the most important job in the world," they always tell me.

C Summarize the reading. Work with a partner and take turns restating the main points. Then work together to write a summary. Include the following:

1. main idea   2. benefit #1   3. benefit #2   4. benefit #3

For additional development of College and Career Readiness skills, see "Disadvantages of Volunteerism," a related reading and activities on pages 108–110.

Lesson E Writing

1 Before you write

A Talk with a partner. Answer the questions.

1. What are some ways to organize your thoughts before writing?

2. Have you ever used an outline or graphic organizer to plan your writing? How did it help you?

B Look at the graphic organizer. This is an example of *clustering*. It includes the main ideas from the reading in Lesson D, "Volunteering While at College."

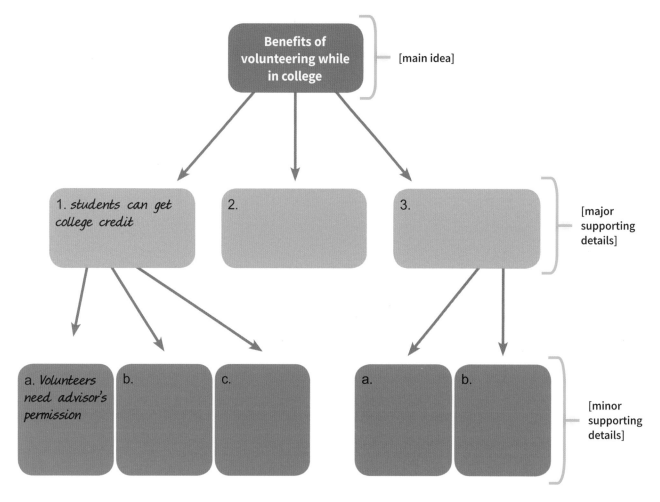

C Work with a partner or partners to complete the chart. Include the key information, but do not write complete sentences. Refer back to the article if you need to.

D **Read** the one-paragraph summary of a two-page government report. Notice these features of the summary:

- The first sentence states the main idea of the article.
- The body sentences summarize the most important supporting details.
- The summary does not include examples.
- Sentences are connected with transitions.
- The summary is paraphrased – written in the writer's words, not the words of the original report.

A U.S. government report on volunteering in America discussed three major trends in 2009. First, the number of Americans who volunteered through formal organizations increased slightly. In contrast, the number of people who volunteered informally by helping their neighbors or serving their local communities went up dramatically. Finally, there was a significant increase in the number of young adults ages 16–24 who volunteered. The report concluded that today's young people have a strong commitment to serving others.

2 Write

Write a one-paragraph summary of the article "Volunteering While at College." Use Exercises 1B, 1C, and 1D to help you.

3 After you write

A **Check** your writing.

	Yes	No
1. I included the main ideas of the article.	☐	☐
2. I included the reasons people choose to volunteer.	☐	☐
3. I included the ways that volunteering can help you get a job.	☐	☐
4. I did not include unnecessary details in my summary.	☐	☐

B **Share** your writing with a partner.

UNIT 4 EFFECTIVE JOB APPLICATIONS

Lesson A Get ready

1 Talk about the pictures

A What are the people in the pictures doing? What do they need to do next?

B What steps do you need to take when applying for a job?

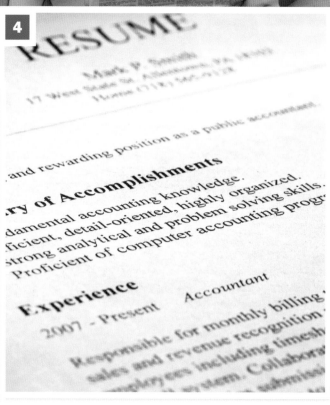

2 Listening

A **Listen** and answer the questions.

1. What was the general topic of the lecture?

2. How many steps does the speaker list? Which connecting words told you the order of the steps?

CD1, Track 11

B **Listen again.** Take notes on the key information.

CD1, Track 11

> Steps in finding a job
> 1.
>
> 2.
>   Best way:
>   Other ways:
>
> 3.
>   Places to find:
>
> 4.
>
> 5.
>
> 6.
>
> 7. Wait for an invitation for an interview
>   While you're waiting:

Listen again. Check your notes. Did you miss anything important?

C **Discuss.** Talk with your classmates.

1. Have you ever applied for a job? What kind of job was it?

2. Which of the steps in the talk have you tried?

3. Who could you use as a reference for a job you are applying for? Why would this person be a good reference for you?

Lesson B Past perfect

1 Grammar focus: Past perfect

The past perfect is formed by *had* + past participle. Use the past perfect to emphasize 1) that one event was completed before another event in the past, or 2) that one past event did not happen until another past event. You can use *before*, *when*, or *by the time* with the later event. (Note: The past perfect is rare in spoken English.)

Watch

> 1st event: John applied for 20 jobs.
> 2nd event: He got his first interview.
>
> **John had applied for 20 jobs by the time he got his first interview.**
>
> 1st event: Pamela never thought about going to college.
> 2nd event: Her high-school counselor suggested it.
>
> **Pamela had never thought about going to college before her high-school counselor suggested it.**

2 Practice

A Write. Read the two events. Make one sentence using the past perfect for the first event.

1. Paul heard about the job. The position was filled.

   By the time _____

2. Mary got a work-study job on campus. She never worked.

   Before _____

3. Isaac worked for his family business. He started his own company.

   Isaac _____ before _____.

4. Carla graduated from high school. She already got her first job.

   When _____

5. Thomas started nursing school. He worked as a medical receptionist.

   Before _____

6. Petra's children grew up and moved out. She got her first job.

   _____ by the time _____.

7. Richard arrived for his job interview. The interviewer already went to lunch.

   When _____

B **Talk** with a partner. Sergei is looking for a job. Yesterday he had an interview at an employment agency. Read the chart and make sentences about the things Sergei completed or didn't complete before the interview.

> Before his interview at the employment agency, Sergei had talked to his friends about job possibilities.

> He hadn't written a résumé.

✓	1. talk to his friends about job possibilities
	2. write a résumé
✓	3. make a list of references
✓	4. ask his previous boss for a letter of recommendation
✓	5. attend a workshop on networking
	6. create a personal website
✓	7. do research online
	8. order business cards
✓	9. buy a new suit

Write sentences about Sergei's job search.

Before his interview at the employment agency, Sergei had talked to his friends about job possibilities.

③ Communicate

A **Make** a list of five important life events that you completed before now. Do not list the events in time order. Include your first job and/or this English course. For example: *got my first job, graduated from high school, got married, became a teacher, got my first apartment.*

B **Exchange** your list with a partner. Ask and answer questions about the events in each other's lives. Use the past perfect.

> **A** Had you gotten married before you got your first job?
> **B** No, I hadn't. / Yes, I had.

C **Share** information about your partner.

Lesson C Reading

1 Before you read

Talk with your classmates. Answer the questions.

1. Have you ever read any ads on a job-search website? What information did the ads ask for?

2. Do you think it's a good idea to apply for jobs you find on the Internet? Why or why not?

2 Read

Read the article. Listen and read again.

CD1, Track 12

ONLINE JOB SEARCHES:

Beware of Scammers!

CONSIDER THESE EXPERIENCES of people applying for jobs on the Internet:

- John applies for a teaching job he found online. He sends in his résumé and some personal information that the employer had requested. Later, John gets a call from his bank saying someone had used the Internet to steal money from his bank account.

- Sophia answers an ad for a salesperson that she saw on a job-search website. She later learns that the information she had given allowed someone to illegally use her credit card number.

These are just two examples of a new way of stealing: using false Internet job listings to gain people's personal information. As more employers see the Internet as an easy and inexpensive way to reach larger numbers of applicants, scammers, or those who use tricks and deception to get private information from people, see an easy way to make money.

Scammers place false ads online to cheat inexperienced job applicants into revealing their personal information.

Believing they are applying for a real job, applicants sometimes give out their social security, student ID, or bank account numbers, their credit card information, or their mother's maiden name. Providing this information allows scammers to steal money from people or make illegal purchases.

The lesson to those who use the Internet to apply for jobs is this: Be cautious! Be wary of online ads that do not mention the company name or that offer a salary that seems too good to be true. These ads may be false.

Before giving any personal information, do some research to see if the company you are dealing with is real. Scammers can set up false websites, so phone, send an email, or visit the office before sending in your résumé. Be careful when you give your personal information to an employer online.

Using the Internet to apply for jobs is convenient, but it is up to you to make sure the job you're applying for is real and the company offering the job is honest.

3 After you read

A **Check** your understanding.

1. What are scammers?

2. What do scammers do to try to cheat people?

3. What are three things you should not put on your application or give online?

4. How can you protect yourself from scammers?

B **Build** your vocabulary. Suffixes change the part of speech of a word. The words in the chart are from the reading. Fill in the missing forms. Use a dictionary if necessary.

Noun	Verb	Adjective	Adverb
1. *applicant, application*	apply		
	legalize	legal, illegal	2.
scammer	3.		
4.	5.	(in)experienced	
6.		(dis)honest	7.

Complete the sentences with the correct form of the words in the chart.

8. Joyce quit her job when she found out that her boss was _____.

9. I didn't get the cashier job because I didn't have any _____ working a cash register.

10. Don't trust anyone who asks for your email password. They are trying to _____ you.

11. The man went to jail after getting hundreds of social security numbers _____.

12. There were more than 300 _____ for the job at the post office.

C **Summarize** the reading. Work with a partner and take turns restating the main points. Then work with your partner to write a summary. Include the following:

1. definition of scammers

2. how scammers cheat job applicants

3. how to protect yourself from scammers

Lesson D Reading

1 Before you read

Talk with your classmates. Answer the questions.

1. Have you ever filled out a job application? What was the job?
2. What kind of information do you think employers want to know about you?

2 Read

Read the article. Listen and read again.

◀)) CD1, Track 13

Ten Tips for a Great Job Application

Why is knowing how to fill out a job application properly so important? For many job seekers, the job application is their letter of introduction. A neatly done, complete application will catch the eye and the interest of a potential new employer, while a messy, incomplete one is much more likely to end up in the trash. Here are ten tips for completing a job application successfully:

1. Be prepared. Collect important documents like your student ID, driver's license, social security number, and résumé, and put these things in a folder for easy access. Also include contact information for your previous employers, your rate of pay, and references.

2. Follow instructions. Take time to read the entire application before you fill it out. Figure out what information is required in each section. Completing the application correctly is the first test of your ability to follow directions.

3. Type accurately. The application is a reflection of you, so be sure to go over it for "typos" and careless grammar mistakes.

4. Target the job. Answer questions with the particular job in mind. Be specific. Include experience and education that matches the requirements of the job that you are applying for.

5. Answer ALL questions. Fill out the application completely; don't leave anything blank. If a question doesn't apply to your situation, write *N/A* or *not applicable*. This will show the employer you are careful.

6. Be honest. Be truthful in the application. Information here will become part of your employment history and, if you lie, someone is sure to find out. You could lose your job. However, do not offer more information than you are asked to give.

7. Don't be negative. Your goal is to get an interview, so play up your strengths and say only positive things about yourself.

8. Salary required. Don't type in a number for salary questions. Instead write "Open." This shows a positive attitude toward discussions about your pay.

9. Gaps in employment. It is OK to have gaps in your work history. Entering information like "returned to school," "moved," or "volunteered" are all acceptable reasons for gaps.

10. Proofread. Reread your application several times before sending it.

Following these guidelines will make it more likely that a potential employer will read your application from beginning to end. A well-done application doesn't guarantee you will get a job, but it certainly increases your chances.

③ **After you read**

A **Check** your understanding. Circle *T* or *F* to indicate whether each statement is true or false.

1. T F Writing specific numbers for salary requirements is advisable.

2. T F You don't need to answer every question on a job application.

3. T F False statements on a job application can cause you to lose your job.

4. T F You should only write positive things about yourself.

5. T F Gaps in your work history should not be mentioned at all on the application.

B **Build** your vocabulary. Many verbs have two parts, a verb and a preposition. These are called *phrasal verbs*. The phrasal verbs below are from the reading. Find and underline them. Then match them with their meanings.

Phrasal verb	Meaning
____ 1. fill out	a. interpret; understand
____ 2. end up	b. complete a printed form
____ 3. figure out	c. review
____ 4. go over	d. arrive at a place, sometimes unexpectedly
____ 5. find out	e. discover

Complete the sentences with a phrasal verb from the list. Change verbs to the past if necessary.

6. Gordon, please _____ the statistics in this report. Something isn't right.

7. I can't go out this weekend. I have to _____ six college applications.

8. The report was disorganized and messy, so I couldn't _____ what the main points were.

9. I just _____ that my boss accepted a job in another state.

10. The painting we received as a wedding gift _____ hanging in our bathroom.

C **Summarize** the reading. Work with a partner and take turns restating the main points. Then work together to write a summary. Include the following:

1. reasons to fill out a job application properly

2. tips for a successful job application

For additional development of College and Career Readiness skills, see "Online Job Applications," a related reading and activities on pages 111–113.

Read a text closely and refer to details and examples to explain what the text says explicitly; determine the meaning of phrasal verbs; summarize a text

Lesson E Writing

1 Before you write

A **Talk** with a partner. Answer the questions.

1. What kind of information should you include in a cover letter?

2. Have you ever written a cover letter? For which job? What did the letter say?

B **Read** Melissa's cover letter.

Melissa Woods   April 14, 2018
4312 Forest Pines Rd.
Columbia, MO 65203
(573) 555-2340
mwoods@cup.org

Dr. Mary Stanford
English Department
Columbia Community College
123 Parkway Avenue
Columbia, MO 65203

Dear Dr. Stanford,

I am applying for the Office Assistant job that was advertised in
the Columbia Community College student newspaper. My résumé
is enclosed.

I am a Spanish language major at the college, and I'm looking for
part-time work on campus. I am available to work ten hours a week, and I
can start immediately.

I don't have any formal work experience yet, but I have been a volunteer
on campus for two large events. I volunteered at the Language Fair in
January 2017 and at the Festival of Books in April 2018. Both of these
were very busy events, and I was able to use my organizational skills to
help make them a success. I coordinated student volunteers and helped
score language exams at the Language Fair, and I filled out important
paperwork for the Festival of Books. Both of these volunteer experiences
helped me learn valuable skills that I can bring to the English Department
office as a student assistant. I am a good writer and I have excellent
computer skills.

I hope you will call or send me an email to schedule an interview. I look
forward to hearing from you soon.

Sincerely,

Melissa Woods
Melissa Woods

C Plan a cover letter for a job at the student store. Fill in the outline with your real or imaginary information.

1. Date: _____

2. Your name, address, phone number, and email: _____

_____

3. Name and title of addressee: _____

4. Job you are interested in: _____

5. How you found out about it: _____

6. Describe yourself. Are you a student or an employee? _____

7. Why are you interested in this job? _____

_____

8. Your job and/or volunteer experience: _____

_____

9. Your skills for this job: _____

2 Write

Write a cover letter for a job you want. Use Exercises 1B and 1C to help you.

3 After you write

A Check your writing.

	Yes	No
1. I included the date and home address.	☐	☐
2. In the first sentence, I wrote the name of the job I'm interested in.	☐	☐
3. I included the reasons I'm interested in this job.	☐	☐
4. I wrote about my job and/or volunteer experiences.	☐	☐

B Share your writing with a partner.

1. Take turns. Read your letter to your partner.

2. Comment on your partner's letter. Did your partner include reasons why he or she wants the job? Did he or she briefly describe himself or herself? Did he or she include his or her job or volunteer experiences?

UNIT 5 SUCCESSFUL INTERVIEWS

Lesson A Get ready

1 Talk about the pictures

A What are "first impressions"?

B Why is it important to make a good first impression on the people you meet?

C What are the people in the photographs doing to create a good/bad first impression?

2 Listening

A Listen and answer the questions.

1. What was the main idea of the talk?

2. What were some interviewing tips that were given in the lecture?

◀)) CD1, Track 14

◀)) CD1, Track 14

B Listen again. Take notes on the key information.

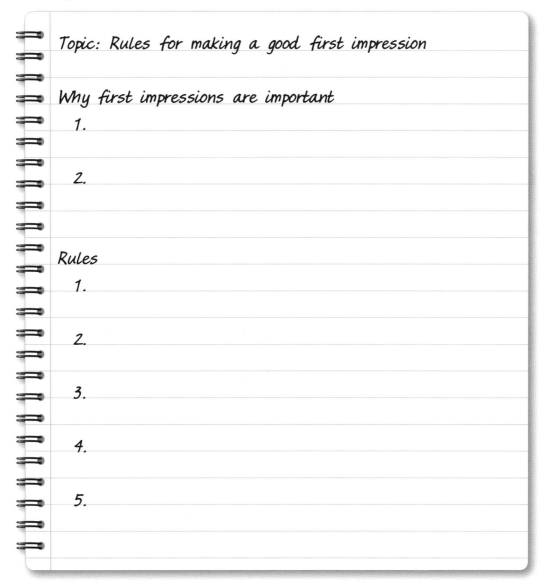

Topic: Rules for making a good first impression

Why first impressions are important

   1.

   2.

Rules

   1.

   2.

   3.

   4.

   5.

Listen again. Check your answers. Did you miss anything important?

C Discuss. Talk with your classmates.

1. Which of the speaker's five rules have you tried?

2. Which rule is the most important, in your opinion?

3. Are these rules the same or different in your native culture? How?

📖 Listen for and identify ways to make a good first impression. **UNIT 5   43**

Lesson B Past modals

1 Grammar focus: *should(n't) have* and *could have*

Should have and *Shouldn't have* + past participle mean that the speaker is sorry about (regrets) something he or she did or did not do in the past. You can also use these modals to comment about another speaker's past actions.

Could have + past participle means that someone had a chance to do something in the past but did not do it. These forms indicate a missed opportunity in the past.

Her interview went badly.	She **should have prepared** better.
She wore jeans to her interview.	She **shouldn't have worn** jeans to the interview.
She didn't have any information about the company before the interview.	She **could have researched** the company online before the interview.

👁 Watch

2 Practice

A **Write** sentences about Akiko using *should have* and *shouldn't have*.

Akiko had a job interview last week. Unfortunately, she didn't get the job.

1. She didn't research the company before the interview.

   She should have researched the company before the interview.

2. She wore casual pants and a T-shirt.

   _____

3. She arrived late. _____

4. She didn't bring a list of references.

   _____

What could Akiko have done differently? Use the cues to make sentences with *could have*.

5. read about the company online

   She could have read about the company online.

6. wear a suit _____

7. leave her house earlier _____

8. email her references before the interview

   _____

B **Talk** with a partner. Read about Sam, John, and Ms. Shue. What should they have done differently? Use *should have* and *shouldn't have*.

> Sam had a personal problem. He asked his boss, Ms. Shue, for a day off to take care of his problem, but she was unsympathetic and would not give it to him. John is Sam's colleague. They often have lunch together and complain about their boss.

Sam

1. didn't talk to John about his problem
2. wrote an angry email about his boss
3. sent the email to John

John

4. accidentally forwarded the email to the whole office, including Ms. Shue
5. didn't pay attention before hitting "Send"

Ms. Shue

6. was not sympathetic to Sam's problem
7. yelled at Sam in front of the whole office

> Sam should have talked to John about his problem. He shouldn't have written an angry email.

Write sentences about different choices Sam, John, and Ms. Shue could have made.

Sam could have tried to talk to his boss again.

8. Sam [try to talk to his boss again]
9. Sam [take care of his problem after work]
10. John [delete Sam's email]
11. Ms. Shue [be more flexible]
12. Ms. Shue [speak to Sam privately]

3 Communicate

A **Work** with a partner. Talk about a mistake you made in the past. Use these phrases:

I should have . . .

I shouldn't have . . .

I could have . . .

> I had a job interview last week. I drove my car to the interview, but there wasn't any parking near the office, so I was late. I should have left my house earlier, and I shouldn't have driven my car. I could have taken the bus.

B **Share** your information with the class.

Lesson C Reading

1 Before you read

Talk with your classmates. Answer the questions.

1. Have you ever interviewed for a job, or at a school or organization?

2. What do you think are some dos and don'ts for a successful interview?

2 Read

Read the article. Listen and read again.

CD1, Track 15

Keys to a Successful Interview

What makes for a successful interview? Consider the experiences of these two job interviewees:

Carlos leaves for a job interview in plenty of time; however, he doesn't consider rush hour traffic and ends up arriving ten minutes late. He opens his bag, sees no papers, and realizes that he left his résumé at home. Carlos is flustered, and while shaking the interviewer's hand, he mispronounces the woman's name.

Sheila takes the time to research the company she is applying to and comes to her interview well prepared. But when the interviewer asks if she had any problems at her last job, she gives a full description of how all her former co-workers were lazy and unmotivated and how she hated working there.

Neither Carlos nor Sheila got the job. Could they have done things differently to get a better outcome?

These scenarios illustrate an important fact: Interviewing skills are essential to creating the kind of positive impression you want to make on the person interviewing you. So instead of thinking about what you should have done to make your last interview go better, consider the following list of important dos and don'ts before your next interview:

DO:

✓ Prepare the materials you need ahead of time.

✓ Arrive early.

✓ Learn the name of the person who is interviewing you.

✓ Learn something about the company, school, or organization beforehand.

✓ Be honest about your skills, education, and experience.

✓ Be positive and interested.

✓ Follow up with a thank-you note.

DON'T:

✗ Wear inappropriate clothing.

✗ Ask about the salary right away.

✗ Be overly nervous.

✗ Speak negatively about others.

✗ Chew gum or smell like smoke.

✗ Act desperate for the position.

3 After you read

A **Check** your understanding.

1. What should Carlos have done to prepare for his interview?

   _____

2. What shouldn't Sheila have done at her interview?

   _____

3. Name three dos and three don'ts for a successful interview.

   _____

B **Build** your vocabulary. Underline the vocabulary words in the article. Use the context to try to guess what they mean. Circle *T* or *F* for the words and their definitions.

1. T   F   An *interviewee* (n.) is a person who is applying for a position.
2. T   F   *Flustered* (adj.) means very calm and relaxed.
3. T   F   A *scenario* (n.) is a story or a series of events.
4. T   F   *Desperate* (adj.) means needing or desiring something very badly.
5. T   F   Something that is suitable or compatible is *inappropriate* (adj.).

Complete the sentences with the correct words.

6. Sheila's comments about her former co-workers were _____ .

7. The employer asked the _____ what her goals for the future were.

8. Even though Steve was _____ for the job, he tried not to show it.

9. In the best interview _____ , both the interviewer and the interviewee
   feel comfortable.

10. Carlos should have been more organized to avoid feeling so _____ .

C **Summarize** the reading. Work with a partner and take turns restating the main points.
Then work together to write a summary. Try to use the vocabulary from Exercise B. Include
the following topics:

1. how to prepare for an interview
2. dos of a successful interview
3. don'ts of a successful interview
4. how to follow up after an interview

Lesson D Reading

1 Before you read

Talk with your classmates. Answer the questions.

1. Have you ever written a thank-you note? In what situation?

2. Why is it important to send a thank-you note after an interview?

2 Read

Read the article. Listen and read again.

CD1, Track 16

MAKE THE MOST OF YOUR INTERVIEW

Follow Up!

Let's say you've just had an interview for an on-campus position or with a new company. Now what? Do you just keep checking your email, waiting by the phone, or searching the mail for a letter offering you the position (or not)? Is there anything more you can do to improve the odds of getting the position?

Unfortunately, chances are that there were dozens, if not hundreds, of other applicants for the job or position to which you just applied. And many of the applicants brought the same kinds of skills, experience, and attitude you did to the interview. So the real question is – How do you make yourself stand out from the crowd?

The answer lies in the realization that the interview is not over when you walk out of the interviewer's office. You must follow up.

Sending a thank-you note after your meeting can help you make the most of your interview. A simple note or email thanking the company for considering you for the position or for the chance to meet some of the people involved is a great way to remind the interviewer that you are truly motivated and interested. It also shows that you have good manners.

A thank-you note is appropriate whether or not you felt the interview was successful. If it went well, a thank-you note may persuade the interviewer to select you over other competing candidates. If it did not go well, the note can help the interviewer remember you favorably even if you are not selected.

At the end of your interview, the interviewer should have told you how to follow up and whom to contact. If not, just address the thank-you note to him or her. Write the note soon after the interview to improve the chance that the interviewer will remember you.

It is important to send only *one* follow-up email or note. If you do not get a response, then you can assume you did not get the position. Don't send any more follow-up notes; you will become an annoyance, and that is not your goal.

Instead, be prepared to move on to the next new opportunity. Don't focus on what could have been, but on what may still lie ahead.

3 After you read

A **Check** your understanding.

1. Why is sending a thank-you note or email important after an interview?

2. Why should you send only one thank-you note as a follow-up?

B **Build** your vocabulary. Match the idioms from the reading with their meanings.

Idiom	Meaning
_____ 1. improve the odds	a. change to a new activity
_____ 2. chances are	b. succeed
_____ 3. stand out from the crowd	c. it is probably true
_____ 4. make the most of	d. increase the possibility
_____ 5. go well	e. make it easy for people to remember you
_____ 6. move on	f. take advantage of

Complete the sentences with the best idiom. Change verb forms if necessary.

7. Improving your computer skills will _____ of your getting a good job.

8. My interview with Professor Schmidt _____. I think there is a good chance that he will select me as his research assistant.

9. Teresa _____ of applicants because of her positive attitude.

10. After losing his job, Jorge was depressed for weeks, but eventually he _____.

11. I don't like my job, but I plan to _____ it.

12. _____ that Gail will move to Washington after she graduates.

C **Summarize** the reading. Work with a partner and take turns restating the main points. Then work together to write a summary. Try to use the vocabulary from Exercise B. Include the following topics:

1. the importance of an interview follow-up

2. what a thank-you note should say

3. why, where, and when to send a thank-you note

For additional development of College and Career Readiness skills, see "Accessing 'Hidden Jobs'," a related reading and activities on pages 114–116.

Read closely to determine what the text says explicitly and to make logical inferences from the text; use context clues to determine the best definition of idioms within a text; summarize a text

Lesson E Writing

1 Before you write

A **Talk** with a partner. Answer the questions.

1. Are thank-you notes after interviews important in your culture?

2. Have you ever written a thank-you note after an interview? What did it say?

B **Read** the different ways of expressing gratitude in a thank-you note.

> **Expressing gratitude**
>
> Thank you for . . .
> I'm very grateful for . . .
> I want to express my gratitude/appreciation for . . .
> I appreciate . . .
> I look forward to working with you / talking with you again.

C **Read** the thank-you email. Underline the expressions of gratitude.

	New Message
To:	Catherine Stevens <c_stevens@cup.org>
Subject:	Thank you for the interview
From:	Ali Bakr
Date:	February 1, 2018 11:56:23 a.m. PST

Dear Ms. Stevens:

Thank you for inviting me to an interview for the position of afternoon shift manager at La Valle Cafeteria. I enjoyed meeting with you and having the opportunity to tell you about my experience and interest in the position. I also enjoyed the facilities tour, and I appreciate the time you spent taking me around. After seeing the kitchen and meeting the student workers, I am excited to think that I might become part of your staff.

Once again, thank you for your help. I look forward to talking with you again soon.

Sincerely,

Ali Bakr

D **Plan** a thank-you email. Complete the chart below with the information that you will include.

Salutation or greeting	
Statement of thanks (include the position you are applying for)	
Specific details about what you liked about the company, school, or organization	
Repetition of thanks and closing remarks	
Signature	

2 Write

Write a thank-you email. Use the information in Exercises 1B, 1C, and 1D to help you.

3 After you write

A **Check** your writing.

	Yes	No
1. I included expressions of gratitude.	☐	☐
2. I thanked the interviewer both in the introduction and in the conclusion.	☐	☐
3. I included specific reasons why I liked the interview.	☐	☐

B **Share** your writing with a partner.

1. Read your partner's note.

2. Who did your partner thank? Why?

UNIT 6 SMALL TALK

Lesson A Get ready

1 Talk about the pictures

A What is small talk? What are some common small-talk topics in the United States?

B What do you think the people in the photos are talking about?

2 Listening

A **Listen** and answer the questions.

1. What is the purpose of small talk?

2. What are some topics that are appropriate for small talk? What are some topics that are inappropriate?

◀)) CD2, Track 2

B **Listen again.** Take notes on the key information.

Topic:

Definition:

   Examples:

Purposes
   1.

   2.

Appropriate topics:

Inappropriate topics:

◀)) CD2, Track 2

Listen again. Check your answers. Did you miss anything important?

C **Discuss.** Talk with your classmates.

1. Have you ever listened to Americans making small talk? What did they talk about?

2. In your culture, how do people start a conversation with people they don't know well? Which topics are safe to talk about?

Lesson B Tag questions

1 Grammar focus: Tag questions

A tag question is a short question that is added to the end of a sentence. Tag questions are used to confirm information or to seek agreement. The tag and the sentence must have the same verb tense. The form is positive sentence + negative tag or negative sentence + positive tag.

Positive sentence + negative tag	Answer	Meaning
It's hot outside, **isn't it**?	Yes, it is.	You agree that it is hot outside.
You like this class, **don't you**?	No, I don't.	You disagree. You don't like the class.

Negative sentence + positive tag	Answer	Meaning
Jane hasn't done the homework, **has she**?	No, she hasn't.	The person who asked the question is correct. Jane has not done the homework.
Lucas didn't get the job, **did he**?	Yes, he did.	The person who asked the question is mistaken. Lucas got the job.

👁 Watch

2 Practice

A **Write.** Make tag questions and answers using the cues.

1. A That was a hard test, _wasn't it_____?

   B _Yes, it was_____. I hope I pass.

2. A Meagan works here, _____?

   B _No, she doesn't_____. She works next door.

3. A Jim was on Facebook, _____?

   B _____. But he's not anymore.

4. A Lida hasn't seen the movie before, _____?

   B _____. She is waiting until she can rent the DVD.

5. A You're going to the meeting, _____?

   B _____. But I have to leave early.

6. A This wasn't written by you, _____?

   B _____. Cindy wrote it.

7. A You're not from Argentina, _____?

   B _____, actually. I'm from Buenos Aires.

B **Talk** with a partner. Make small talk by asking and answering tag questions.

A You're from Korea, aren't you?

B No, I'm not. I'm from Thailand.

Student A

You think that your partner . . .

1. is from _____ (country)

2. came to the United States last year

3. is married

4. has two children

5. didn't come to class yesterday

6. is going to work right after class

7. can't speak Spanish

8. will be in class tomorrow

Student B

You think that your partner . . .

1. is from _____ (country)

2. just bought a car

3. isn't married

4. has a dog

5. didn't go to work yesterday

6. is going to move to _____ (state)

7. can't sing

8. is leaving early today

3 Communicate

A **Write** six sentences about yourself – three that are true and three that are not true. Exchange papers with a partner. Use your partner's sentences to ask tag questions. Answer your partner's questions.

B **Work** with a partner. Role-play a conversation between two people who are making small talk at a party. Begin with a tag question. End the conversation politely. Begin your conversation with a comment about one of these topics:

- the weather or room temperature

- the party, the room, the food, the host, or the music

- where you've seen the other person before

A It's hot in here, isn't it?

B Yes, it sure is.

A Are you from around here?

B No, I'm actually from _____.

A Me, too. We have a lot to talk about!

B Oh, I'd love to continue this conversation, but I've got to go now.

A Oh, sorry to hear that. Take care.

B Bye!

C **Perform** your role play for the class.

Lesson C Reading

1 Before you read

Talk with your classmates. Answer the questions.

1. The article below is called "Small Talk, Big Problems." What do you think it's about?

2. Have you ever had problems with understanding small talk?

2 Read

Read the article. Listen and read again.

CD2, Track 3

Small Talk, Big Problems

Marco, a new immigrant from Chile, works in a factory during the day and takes college classes at night. Shortly after starting at work and at school, he has two confusing experiences:

- One evening, he sees an American student from one of his classes walking toward him. As the student comes closer, Marco says, "Hi." The student responds with "Hi, how are you?" But instead of waiting for Marco's answer, the student keeps on walking. Marco is confused and wonders, "Why does my classmate dislike me?"
- At the factory, Marco sits down to have lunch with a group of co-workers. He introduces himself and talks a bit about his family, and his co-workers do the same. At the end of lunch, an American co-worker says, "It was nice to meet you, Marco. Let's get together sometime." A week goes by. Marco sees the woman every day, but she never talks about seeing him or getting together with him outside of work. Marco wonders, "Why did she lie to me?"

Are Marco's conclusions correct? Does his classmate dislike him? Is his co-worker a liar? In both cases, no. Neither the classmate nor the colleague was trying to be rude.

The problem in these scenarios was that Marco was unaware of the difference between the speakers' *words* and their *intentions*. Marco did not know that "How are you?", "Let's get together," and similar expressions are actually a form of small talk. "How are you?" and "How are you doing?" are not real questions. They are greetings, similar to "Hello." A speaker who uses these expressions does not expect an answer beyond "Fine, thanks."

Likewise, "Let's keep in touch," "I'll call you," or "Let's talk soon" are not invitations or promises to get in touch. They are simply polite ways of closing a conversation.

But if Americans don't mean what they say, how can you know when they are truly interested in knowing about your health or when they're sincerely looking forward to meeting you again? Watch their behavior. If the speaker makes eye contact and waits to hear your answer, chances are they are asking a real question. In the second case, you can recognize a real invitation if the speaker makes an appointment with you for a specific day and time.

The lesson to learn from Marco's experiences is that it isn't always enough to understand the words that people use. You have to know the intention, or purpose, behind them as well.

3 After you read

A **Check** your understanding.

1. What was the cause of Marco's misunderstandings?

2. What are some examples of small talk phrases that are often misunderstood?

3. How should you respond if an American says "How are you?" or "Let's keep in touch"?

B **Build** your vocabulary.

1. English has many verb + preposition + *-ing* combinations. It can be difficult to remember which prepositions to use. Fill in the missing prepositions in the combinations below. Then write an explanation or synonym for each combination. Use a dictionary if necessary.

Preposition combination	Definition
1. keep _____ (walking)	*continue*
2. talk _____ (seeing)	
3. be guilty _____ (lying)	
4. be interested _____ (knowing)	
5. look forward _____ (meeting)	

2. Write your own sentences with the verb + preposition + *-ing* combinations.

C **Summarize** the reading. Work with a partner and take turns restating the main points. Then work together to write a summary. Try to use the vocabulary from Exercise B. Include the following topics:

1. the cause of Marco's misunderstandings

2. examples of expressions that don't mean what they sound like

3. how to know when Americans mean what they say

4. the lesson to learn from Marco's experiences

Lesson D Reading

1 Before you read

Talk with your classmates. Answer the questions.

1. What are some places where small talk can happen?

2. Have you ever met someone interesting through small talk? Where were you?

2 Read

Read the article. Listen and read again.

🔊 CD2, Track 4

Strategies for Successful Small Talk

Opportunities for small talk can happen anywhere: on an airplane, in the school cafeteria, in line for a concert, or before an office meeting. But how do you start a conversation, how do you end it politely, and what should you do in between? Below are tips that will help you fit in just about anywhere.

1 Prepare a list of neutral conversation starters that you can call on in any situation. "Excuse me" is always a good way to get someone's attention before you engage them with a question such as "Do you have the time?", "Where's the bus stop?", or "It's not supposed to rain, is it?"

2 Learn phrases for exiting from conversations gracefully. Useful expressions include "It's been great talking to you, but I really have to go," "It was nice talking to you," or "Excuse me, I have to . . ." As you are walking away, you can add "Take care," "See you later," or "Take it easy."

3 Work on your listening skills and practice making listening sounds. "I see," "Yes, of course," "Uh-huh," "Really," or "Wow!" show you are listening and focused on what the other person is saying.

4 Use positive body language. Use a mirror to practice smiling, making eye contact, and nodding. Americans will interpret these behaviors as signals that you are paying attention.

5 Learn how to interrupt politely. Say "Excuse me," "Pardon me," or "Sorry," and then follow up with a question about what the speaker has just said. In American culture, it is not always rude to cut in when another person is speaking; on the contrary, interrupting sometimes shows that you are actively involved in the conversation.

6 Write down funny stories you hear or interesting experiences you've had. Then practice saying them aloud. Telling a funny story is an excellent way to break the ice.

7 Most of all, don't be shy! In the United States, it is normal to start up a casual conversation with someone you've never met before. So the next time you're standing in line at the supermarket, don't be afraid to say to the person in front of you, "Nice day, isn't it?"

③ After you read

A **Check** your understanding.

1. How can you prepare yourself to make small talk?

2. Imagine you are a passenger on an airplane, and the person sitting next to you just took a break from reading a book. What could you say to make small talk?

3. Of the seven tips, which have you already tried? Which do you plan to try next?

B **Build** your vocabulary.

1. A phrasal verb is a verb plus a preposition or adverb which creates a meaning different from the meaning of the original verb. Form phrasal verbs by drawing lines from the verb to the preposition/adverb. Then write the meanings.

Verb	Preposition/ Adverb	Meaning
1. fit	on	
2. call	in	*be accepted by the people you're with*
3. focus	down	
4. follow	up	
5. write	on	
6. start	up	

2. Work with a partner. Form your own sentence with each of the phrasal verbs.

C **Summarize** the reading. Work with a partner and take turns restating the main points. Then work together to write a summary. Try to use the vocabulary from Exercise B. Include the following topics:

1. places or situations where small talk is common

2. phrases for making and ending small talk

3. listening sounds and body language

4. how to interrupt politely

For additional development of College and Career Readiness skills, see "Making the Best of Small Talk," a related reading and activities on pages 117–119.

Determine the central idea of a text and how reasons and examples support it; recognize and determine meaning of phrasal verbs and use them appropriately; summarize a text

Lesson E Writing

1 Before you write

A **Talk** with your classmates. Answer the questions.

1. Review what you learned in Lesson A (page 53) about appropriate and inappropriate topics for small talk in the United States. Give examples of questions you should and shouldn't ask.

2. How is small talk in your country the same as in the United States? How is it different?

B **Make** a list in your notebook of appropriate and inappropriate small-talk topics in your culture.

C **Complete** the diagrams.

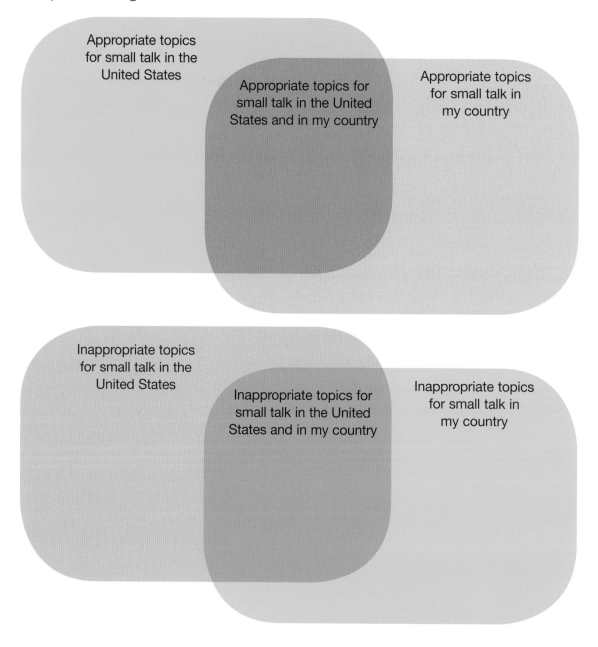

Appropriate topics for small talk in the United States

Appropriate topics for small talk in the United States and in my country

Appropriate topics for small talk in my country

Inappropriate topics for small talk in the United States

Inappropriate topics for small talk in the United States and in my country

Inappropriate topics for small talk in my country

D **Plan** a paragraph comparing appropriate and inappropriate topics for small talk in the United States and in your country. Use the outline in the chart as a guide; you may change words and add or delete topics or examples according to the information you want to include.

Topic sentence	*Appropriate and inappropriate small talk topics in the United States and _____ (your country) are mostly (similar/different).*
Similarities	• topics that are appropriate in both cultures • examples of common questions
Differences	• topics that are inappropriate in the United States, but acceptable in my culture • examples
	• topics that are appropriate in the United States, but unacceptable in my culture • examples
Conclusion	*These are just a few examples of how small talk topics are similar and different in the United States and in my country.*

2 Write

Write a paragraph comparing appropriate and inappropriate topics for small talk in the United States and in your country. Use Exercises 1A, 1B, 1C, and 1D to help you.

3 After you write

A **Check** your writing.

	Yes	No
1. I wrote a topic sentence expressing my main idea.	☐	☐
2. I wrote about similarities between the United States and my country.	☐	☐
3. I wrote about differences between the United States and my country.	☐	☐
4. I wrote a conclusion for my paragraph.	☐	☐

B **Share** your writing with a partner.

1. Take turns. Read your writing to your partner.

2. Comment on your partner's writing. Ask your partner questions. Tell your partner one thing you learned.

UNIT 7 IMPROVING RELATIONSHIPS

Lesson A Get ready

1 Talk about the pictures

A Are the people in the pictures working alone or in groups? Is this the best way for them to work, in your opinion?

B What is teamwork? Why is it important at work and school?

2 Listening

A **Listen** and answer the questions.

1. What is the definition of teamwork?

2. Why is teamwork important?

3. According to the speaker, what is one benefit of teamwork?

◀)) CD2, Track 5

B **Listen again.** Take notes on the key information.

◀)) CD2, Track 5

Topic:

Definition:

Importance
   For organizations:
   For individuals:

Benefits
   1. Increased employee/student involvement
   2.
   3.
   4.

Conclusion
   In the past:
   Today:

Listen again. Check your notes. Did you miss anything important?

C **Discuss.** Talk with your classmates.

1. Why do you think teamwork reduces absenteeism?

2. How do you think teamwork reduces costs in an organization?

3. In your country, is it common for students and workers to work in teams?

4. Do you enjoy working on teams at school or work? Why or why not?

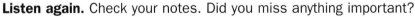

Lesson B Unreal conditionals

1 Grammar focus: The present unreal conditional

Conditional sentences consist of a dependent clause and a main clause. The dependent clause begins with *if*. The main clause uses *would*, *could*, or *might* + verb. Use the present unreal conditional to talk about imaginary situations in the present or to give advice. Use a comma after an *if*-clause at the beginning of a sentence.

Watch

Example	Explanation
If we had more time, we **could do** a better job.	We don't have enough time, so we can't do a good job.
We **could finish** this project faster **if** we had more people on our team.	We don't have enough people on our team, so we can't work quickly.
If I **were** you, I **would talk** to the boss about the problem.	You should talk to the boss about the problem.

In formal English, the form of the *be*-verb in the dependent clause is *were* for all subjects. In conversation it is acceptable to say *If I was* or *If he/she was*.

2 Practice

A Write. Complete the sentences. Use the present unreal conditional. Use *would*, *could*, or *might* in the main clause.

1. At the ZZ Mattress Company, we don't work in teams. If we (work) _____*worked*_____ in teams, we (save) ____*might save*____ time.

2. We don't have enough space in our office. Maybe the workers (be) _____ more patient with each other if we (have) _____ more space.

3. My office mate talks on his cell phone all the time. I (concentrate) _____ better if he (talk) _____ outside.

4. Our manager is not a good communicator. If our manager (be) _____ a better communicator, we (not have) _____ trouble following directions.

5. Jim's manager does not trust him. Jim (be) _____ more motivated to work hard if his manager (trust) _____ him.

6. I'm sorry you're having problems with your team leader. If I (be) _____ you, I (join) _____ a different team.

7. Carmen does not work well in teams. If I (be) _____ her manager, I (not force) _____ her to work with other people.

B Talk with a partner. Read the paragraph and the sentences about Peter. Make sentences about the imaginary situations. Use the present unreal conditional.

> Peter is a teaching assistant in a large class. He got the job because he is smart and he knows the material well. But there are several problems in his class.
>
> Peter is shy, so he doesn't relate well to the students.

> But if he weren't shy, he could relate well to the students.

1. He speaks softly, so the students can't hear him.

2. He never asks any questions, so the students don't need to pay attention.

3. He does not use interesting examples, so his lectures are boring.

4. The students don't respect him, so they come to class late.

5. There are no rules for behavior, so the students use their cell phones and text during class.

6. His tests are easy, so the students are not challenged.

7. His department chair never observes his class, so she doesn't know about the problems.

Write sentences about Peter. Use the present unreal conditional.

If Peter spoke more loudly, the students could hear him.

3 Communicate

Work in small groups. Take turns reading the situations and giving advice. Use *If I were you . . .* for advice.

1. You and three other students are assigned to do a research project for your business class. One student in the group is not doing his share of the work. You're worried that your project will be late because of him, and you will get a lower grade.

> If I were you, I would speak to the professor about the problem.

2. You're working with a committee to plan a dinner honoring your children's teacher, who is retiring. One person on the committee is very bossy. She is always telling everyone else what to do. You like this woman, but it's hard for you to work with her.

3. Your boss assigned a project to you and three other workers. He gave you a deadline, but no directions about how to divide up the work. You've never worked on a team before, and you don't know how to begin.

Lesson C Reading

1 Before you read

Talk with your classmates. Answer the questions.

1. What are some annoying or disruptive behaviors at work or in school?

2. Who is responsible for protecting students or workers from disruptive or abusive behavior?

2 Read

Read the article. Listen and read again.

 CD2, Track 6

BAD BEHAVIOR IN THE WORKPLACE

A recent survey by Randstad USA, an employer staffing firm, asked over 1,500 U.S. employees to identify the things co-workers do that they find most annoying. Number one on the list of the seven worst behaviors was gossiping, the passing around of rumors and intimate information.

Other employee pet peeves included wasting company time with poor time-management skills; colleagues who leave messes in common areas, such as the lunch or meeting rooms; unpleasant scents and loud noises in the office; overuse of phones and laptops in meetings; and misuse of company email (for example, emailing too often or copying too many people on messages).

But the list of bothersome behaviors in the workplace did not end there. It included abusive behaviors like bullying and sexual harassment. An earlier survey done by the online learning provider SkillSoft found bullying by co-workers and management to be a top employee concern.

Bullying is defined as behavior done by a person with greater power for the purpose of intimidating, or frightening, a weaker or less powerful person. The term *bully* is usually associated with a child who behaves badly, but a manager who repeatedly criticizes a worker in front of co-workers, or a professor who ridicules a student's religious beliefs or appearance, may also be guilty of bullying.

Sexual harassment – which includes inappropriate touching or sexual remarks and using threats to force unwanted sexual activity on an employee or fellow student – is a serious workplace abuse. Both males and females can be targets of sexual harassment.

Both bullying and sexual harassment are against the law. All government and state offices, as well as colleges, have written policies that define and prohibit these behaviors. So do most large companies. The U.S. Equal Employment Opportunity Commission, or EEOC, is the government agency in charge of enforcing laws against discrimination, which includes sexual harassment.

Annoying colleagues, bad work etiquette, and abusive behavior can all lead to unhappy working conditions that affect worker productivity and satisfaction. Well-managed organizations have rules and procedures in place to define improper behavior and prevent these abuses.

3 After you read

A **Check** your understanding.

1. What are some examples of employee pet peeves? Do these things annoy you, too?

2. What is an example of bullying at work? Can you think of any others?

3. What advice would you give a classmate who was being bullied? Start with *If I were you . . .*

4. What is sexual harassment?

B **Build** your vocabulary.

1. English uses punctuation, phrases, and clauses to signal definitions in a text. Look for the following expressions in the reading and complete the chart.

Expression	Definition signal	Definition
1. gossiping	a comma between two nouns ("gossiping" and "passing")	the passing around of rumors and intimate information
2. pet peeves		
3. common areas		
4. misuse of company email		
5. abusive behaviors		
6. bullying		
7. intimidating		
8. sexual harassment		

2. Use each expression from the chart in an original sentence about your workplace, school, or volunteer organization.

C **Summarize** the reading. Work with a partner and take turns restating the main points. Then work together to write a summary. Try to use the vocabulary from Exercise B. Include the following topics:

1. findings of the Randstad USA survey

2. finding of the SkillSoft study

3. examples of bullying and sexual harassment

4. the EEOC

Lesson D Reading

1 Before you read

Talk with your classmates. Answer the questions.

1. Has anyone ever annoyed you at work or school? How did you deal with it?

2. What do you think is the best way to deal with annoying people?

2 Read

Read the article. Listen and read again.

CD2, Track 7

Don't Let Annoying People Drive You Nuts

How many times have you had to put up with a phone ringing in someone's pocket in class, the loud talker in the seat behind you on a plane, or the choking smell of perfume in the office meeting room? When someone's behavior annoys you, what do you do? Well, if you don't know the offending person or aren't tied to the situation, you can get up and leave. But what if you can't leave, or if you're forced to share space with a person who regularly drives you up a wall – what then?

Getting Angry Isn't the Answer
Experts in group relations say that getting angry with an annoying person only makes a bad situation worse. A confrontation can put you in a bad mood, increase your stress level, and make you say things that you might regret later. However, turning a blind eye to the problem and doing nothing will only make you more resentful, and it won't make things better.

The Direct Approach Is Often the Best
If you decide the problem is bad enough, and if you can't avoid it by changing office desks or moving to a different part of the classroom, many experts agree that addressing the problem head-on is your best approach. But be careful. If you sound overly critical or accusatory, your attempt to clear the air might backfire and make matters worse.

Instead of criticizing, experts suggest a more constructive approach. First, try to take into account the other person's feelings. He or she may not be aware of their annoying behavior. Just letting the person know your point of view – without criticizing or putting blame on them – is a healthy approach. Use "I" language instead of "you" language. For example, saying "I would appreciate your keeping your voice down a little" sounds much less accusatory and mean-spirited than "You talk so loud, I can't hear myself think."

If the annoyance is minor, like a colleague whose gum chewing grates on your nerves, don't make a big deal out of it. An indirect or joking comment may be sufficient: "Hey, I guess that gum tastes really good! But I'm having trouble concentrating – could you please chew more quietly?"

In short, when it comes to dealing with annoying classmates or co-workers, a little diplomacy goes a long way.

3 After you read

A Check your understanding.

1. Why is it not helpful to get angry with annoying people?

2. What does the writer mean by a "direct" approach?

3. What is "I" language? Give an example.

4. A friend is annoyed with a colleague who often uses office email to send around photos of her family. What advice would you give your friend? Start with *If I were you . . .*

B Build your vocabulary.

1. Complete the idioms in the chart using words from the reading.

2. Work with a partner. Write a synonym or explanation for each idiom.

Idiom	Explanation
1. _____drive_____ you nuts	*To irritate or annoy very much*
2. drive you up a _____	
3. in a bad _____	
4. turning a _____ eye	
5. address a problem _____ on	
6. clear the _____	
7. take into _____	
8. grate on your _____	
9. make a big _____ out of something	

3. Work with your partner to write a short conversation. Use two idioms from the chart. Role-play your conversation for the class.

C Summarize the reading. Work with a partner and take turns restating the main points. Then work together to write a summary. Try to use the vocabulary from Exercise B. Include the following topics:

1. examples of annoying behaviors

2. why you shouldn't get angry

3. ways of approaching annoying people in a positive way

For additional development of College and Career Readiness skills, see "Strategies for Dealing with Bad Behavior," a related reading and activities on pages 120–122.

Lesson E Writing

1 Before you write

A **Talk** with your classmates. Answer the questions.

1. Do you ever read advice columns in newspapers, magazines, or online?

2. Have you ever written a letter asking for advice? Did you get a response? Did you follow the advice you received?

B **Read** the letter and response in a workplace advice column.

Workplace Advice

Dear Brenda,

    I have an embarrassing problem. I really don't know how to deal with it. My office mate has very strong body odor. It has gotten to the point where I cannot stand to be in my office anymore. I have tried leaving the door open, but it doesn't work. I've been spending most of my day in the next office, but this is not ideal because I feel like I am crowding out the people who work there. My co-worker is a very nice person. What would you do if you were me?

    — Desperate for Air, New York, NY

Dear Desperate,

    That situation sounds very awkward. No one likes to hear that they smell bad. If I were you, I would put together a nice package of personal cleansing items like soap, deodorant, and a washcloth. I would wrap the package and give it to my office mate as a gift. I would explain that I am very sensitive to strong smells, and that I would appreciate it if she used these items. Try to speak gently and calmly. Explain that you enjoy sharing an office with her, and that this will help you work together better. If this solution does not work, ask your supervisor to move you to a different office. Explain that your current office environment is interfering with your ability to concentrate on your work. I respect your effort to take your office mate's feelings into account, but your first responsibility is to perform your job duties as effectively as possible.

    — Brenda

C **Work** with a partner. Answer the questions about Brenda's response.

1. What information does the advice columnist write at the beginning of her response?

2. How many solutions does the advice columnist suggest?

3. What grammar and expressions does the columnist use to give advice?

D **Plan** a response to a letter asking for advice about an annoying problem at work or school.

1. Choose a problem to respond to. It can be a real problem you've had at work or school, or it can be one of the problems in the readings on pages 66 and 68. Summarize the problem here:

   _____

   _____

   _____

   _____

   _____

2. Imagine you are an advice columnist. Brainstorm solutions to the problem.

   Solution 1: _____

   _____

   Solution 2: _____

   _____

   Solution 3: _____

   _____

2 Write

Write a paragraph in which you respond to a letter asking for advice about an annoying problem at school or work. Include at least two solutions. Use Exercises 1B, 1C, and 1D to help you.

3 After you write

A **Check** your writing.

	Yes	No
1. I referred to the problem in the first one or two sentences of my response.	☐	☐
2. I suggested at least two solutions.	☐	☐
3. I used *If I were you* and imperative verbs to give advice.	☐	☐

B **Share** your writing with a partner.

1. Take turns. Explain the problem to your partner. Then read your response.

2. Respond to your partner's writing. Do you agree with the advice your partner gave?

Lesson A Get ready

1 Talk about the pictures

A What is criticism? Is criticism always negative?

B What kind of criticism do you think the people in the photos received?

2 Listening

A **Listen** and answer the questions.

1. Who criticized Ray? Why? How?

2. What was Ray's response?

3. What is the difference between negative criticism and constructive criticism?

 CD2, Track 8

B **Listen again.** Take notes on the key information.

 CD2, Track 8

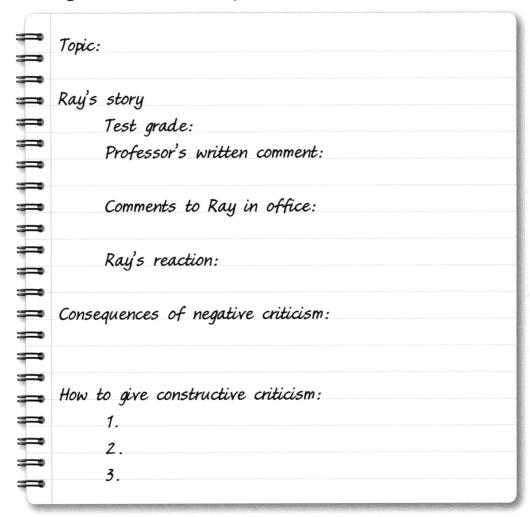

Topic:

Ray's story
     Test grade:
     Professor's written comment:

     Comments to Ray in office:

     Ray's reaction:

Consequences of negative criticism:

How to give constructive criticism:
     1.
     2.
     3.

Listen again. Check your answers. Did you miss anything important?

C **Discuss.** Talk with your classmates.

1. According to the three steps of giving constructive criticism, what should Ray's professor have done differently?

2. Have you ever been in a situation where you felt you were criticized unfairly? What did you do to resolve the situation?

Lesson B Conditional clauses

1 Grammar focus: The past unreal conditional

The past unreal conditional expresses opinions or wishes about situations that were unreal (not true) in the past. The verb forms are *had* + past participle in the dependent clause and *would/could/might (not)* + *have* + past participle in the main clause. Use a comma after an *if*-clause at the beginning of a sentence.

Example	Explanation
If Ray **had studied** more for the test, he **would have gotten** a higher score.	Ray got a low score on the test because he didn't study enough.
Ray **wouldn't have done** so badly on the test if he **had gone** to a study session.	Ray didn't go to a study session. He did badly on the test.

👁 Watch

2 Practice

A **Write.** Complete the sentences. Use the past unreal conditional.

1. Tom didn't receive the email about the staff meeting, so he didn't go. If Tom (receive)
   ___*had received*___ the email, he (go) *would have gone* to the meeting.

2. Donna forgot to put gas in her car. She ran out of gas and was late to class. She (not be)
   _____ late if she (remember) _____ to put gas in her car.

3. Steve turned in his paper late. He got a bad grade. Steve (get) _____ a
   better grade if he (turn in) _____ his paper on time.

4. Tina wrote her report too quickly. Her boss made her rewrite it. If Tina (write)
   _____ her report more carefully, her boss (not make)
   _____ her do it again.

5. Jim yelled at his boss. His boss got upset. If Jim (not yell) _____ at his
   boss, his boss (not get) _____ upset.

6. Jack needed more time to finish his project. He asked Boutros to help him. He (not finish)
   _____ the project on time if Boutros (not help) _____
   him.

7. George's English class didn't have a year-end party. The students didn't get a chance to
   say good-bye to each other. If the class (have) _____ a year-end party,
   the students (have) _____ a chance to say good-bye.

B **Talk** with a partner. Read about Mario. Use the cues to make sentences about what would or could have happened if the situation had been different.

Mario recently got a job in a busy office. The work is challenging, but Mario is satisfied because he's learning new skills. His boss is demanding but fair.

Yesterday Mario had a hard day. His boss assigned him an important project to do by himself.

If the boss hadn't trusted Mario, he wouldn't have assigned him an important project.

1. The boss trusted Mario, so he assigned him an important project.
2. The project had a tight deadline. Mario worried about finishing on time.
3. Mario didn't feel confident because he didn't have a colleague to consult.
4. Mario needed to work overtime because there were problems.
5. Mario's desk was full of papers, so he lost an important document.
6. Mario's computer crashed, so he lost some data.
7. Mario finished the project on time because he stayed up all night.
8. The boss was pleased because Mario finished the project on time.

Write sentences about Mario. Use the past unreal conditional.

If the boss hadn't trusted Mario, he wouldn't have assigned him an important project.

3 Communicate

A **Write** a list of five things you are sorry that you did or did not do at work or school. Say what happened as a result.

I lent my lecture notes to Linda and she lost them.

B **Work** with a partner. Take turns reading and responding to your sentences from A. Use the past unreal conditional in your responses.

A I lent my lecture notes to Linda and she lost them.

B That's too bad. If you hadn't lent your notes to Linda, she wouldn't have lost them.

A You're right. In the future I won't lend my notes to anyone.

C **Share** information about your partner with the class.

Lesson C Reading

1 Before you read

Talk with your classmates. Answer the questions.

1. What do you think "accepting criticism gracefully" means?
2. Why is it important to accept criticism this way?

2 Read

Read the article. Listen and read again.

 CD2, Track 9

ACCEPTING CRITICISM GRACEFULLY

Accepting criticism gracefully is not an easy thing to do. Criticism can be extremely hurtful and can make us feel exposed and vulnerable. In her article "Handling Criticism with Honesty and Grace," communications expert Kare Anderson offers some insights into why criticism makes us feel so bad and how to lessen the pain.

Anderson states that criticism is so powerful because when we receive it, we are like animals under attack. "Your heart beats faster [and] your skin temperature goes down . . . your instincts are to focus on that feeling," which makes it stronger. Criticism, she adds, makes people want to either run away or fight back.

Anderson says it is important to focus on the content of the critical comments and not to let defensive emotions build up inside us. Putting up defenses may lead us to take "a superior or righteous position, get more rigid, and listen less as the criticism continues."

Anderson encourages people to follow a four-step process when responding to criticism.

1 Step one is to show, either verbally or with a simple nod, that you heard the criticism. Staying calm and saying something like "I understand how concerned you are about this" is much better than saying "You are totally wrong" or "You don't know what you are talking about."

2 Step two is to ask for more information, even if you disagree with the criticism. This will help both parties understand the message. Anderson says, "The more fully the [critical] person feels heard, the more likely he or she will be receptive to your response."

3 In step three, both parties should seek to find something they can agree on in the message. Usually there is some kernel of truth in criticism. Take responsibility for at least that much. If there is nothing at all to agree upon, however, look at the positive intentions of the critical party, saying something like "I understand your need to be very thorough." or "If I had known how much you cared about the project, . . ."

4 Step four is responding to the criticism, but always after asking permission first. If you disagree with the criticism, you can say, "May I give you my opinion?" or "What can we do to make things better?" However, Anderson says, "if [on the other hand] you believe the [critical] comments are accurate, say so. If an apology is in order, give it sooner rather than later."

3 After you read

A **Check** your understanding.

1. How do most people typically feel when someone criticizes them?

2. When someone criticizes you, why is it important to focus on the content of the criticism?

3. What steps should people follow when responding to criticism, according to Anderson?

4. Imagine your teacher criticized your essay because it is too long. You disagree. What could you say to your teacher according to each of Anderson's four steps?

B **Build** your vocabulary.

1. Read the words in the chart that end in -ly. These words are *adverbs*. They modify verbs, adjectives, other adverbs, and whole sentences.

2. Find and underline the expressions with adverbs in the reading. In the chart, check the form that the adverbs modify.

Expressions with adverbs	Verb	Adjective	Adverb	Whole sentence
1. accepting criticism *gracefully*	✓			
2. *extremely* hurtful				
3. show *verbally*				
4. you are *totally* wrong				
5. the more *fully* the person feels heard				
6. *Usually* there is some kernel				

3. Work with a partner. Choose one adverb from the chart and form your own sentence in which the adverb modifies a verb, an adjective, another adverb, or a whole sentence.

C **Summarize** the reading. Work with a partner and take turns restating the main points. Then work together to write a summary. Try to use the vocabulary from Exercise B. Include the following topics:

1. why criticism affects people strongly

2. the four steps of receiving and responding to criticism

3. the importance of focusing on the message – not your feelings

Lesson D Reading

1 Before you read

Talk with your classmates. Answer the questions.

1. In which situations do people normally receive evaluations (written or spoken) of their performance?

2. Have you ever had a performance evaluation? In which situation? How did you deal with criticism, if any?

2 Read

Read the article. Listen and read again.

The Performance Evaluation

◀) CD2, Track 10

Serena was sitting in the office cafeteria reading the newspaper when her friend John walked in. He looked rather sad. John poured himself a cup of coffee and walked over to her. "Hi," he said, slumping down into a chair.

Serena looked up from her paper. "Looks like things didn't go well with your evaluation," she said.

"Nope, it was awful."

"What happened?" she asked.

"I messed up," said John. "I lost my cool when Bill said some things about my performance I didn't agree with."

"Why did you do that?" asked Serena.

"I don't know really. I felt hurt, I guess, and embarrassed."

Serena put down her paper. "What exactly did he say?"

"Well, first," said John, "he said I need to use my time better, you know, stop chitchatting so much with co-workers because I wasn't working fast enough." John looked up at her. "Just hearing it started my heart racing and all I could think about was how bad it made me feel. Then he said a few more negative things."

"What more did he say?"

"You know," answered John, "I'm not really sure. I can't remember now."

"You can't remember . . . weren't you listening?" asked Serena.

"Well, yes and no . . . you see, I started to get all defensive and started talking about what a good job I do and how much I disagreed with him." John shook his head. "Then I started blabbing about my workload and how the other folks in my department aren't pulling their weight."

"You started blaming others?" said Serena.

"Yeah, I know," John said, looking over at her. "Bad, huh?" He drank his coffee and stared into his cup. "I was so surprised and embarrassed, I just blew up."

John thought for a moment, then said, "I wish I could do it over again. If I had known he was so displeased with my work, I would have been more prepared for the criticism. Maybe I would have been more calm."

John suddenly stood up.

"Where are you going?" asked Serena.

"First I'm going to email Bill an apology and ask for another meeting," he said, sliding his chair beneath the table, "and then I'm getting back to work."

3 After you read

A   **Check** your understanding.

1.   What did Bill say about John's performance?

2.   How did John react to his boss's criticism?

3.   If John had known that his boss was displeased, how would he have behaved differently?

4.   What is John going to do next?

B   **Build** your vocabulary.

1.   The expressions in the chart are examples of *slang*, or informal language. Slang is common in casual conversation; you should not use it in formal speaking situations or when you write. Look for the expressions in the reading and underline them.

2.   Look up the expressions in a dictionary. Write formal synonyms or definitions in the chart.

Slang expression	Formal synonym/definition
1. nope	*no*
2. mess up	
3. lose one's cool	
4. chitchat	
5. blab	
6. pull one's weight	
7. blow up	

3.   Work with a partner. Role-play short conversations (two or three lines) using the slang expressions. Then write sentences using the formal synonyms.

C   **Summarize** the reading. Work with a partner and take turns restating the main points. Then work together to write a summary. Try to use the vocabulary from Exercise B. Include the following topics:

1.   Bill's criticism of John's performance

2.   how John felt

3.   what John said

4.   John's feelings now

5.   what John plans to do next

For additional development of College and Career Readiness skills, see "Problems with Performance Reviews," a related reading and activities on pages 123–125.

Cite textual evidence to draw inferences from a text; use a dictionary to identify formal synonyms for informal expressions in a text; summarize a text

Lesson E Writing

1 Before you write

A **Talk** with your classmates. Answer the questions.

1. Think of a time when you received criticism. Who criticized you – a teacher, a supervisor, a family member, an acquaintance, or a stranger?

2. Was the criticism negative or constructive?

3. How did you react to the criticism?

4. Did you change as a result of the criticism? How?

B **Read** the story.

An Educational Experience

The summer after I graduated from high school I traveled to Paris, France. I had studied French for three years in high school and I had always gotten good grades. I thought my French was pretty good, and I was very excited about going to France and trying out the language there.

On my first day, I went to a café and ordered a café au lait. As soon as the waiter heard my French, he started to laugh and make jokes about Americans and their funny accents. I was devastated. I got so flustered that I couldn't remember another word in French. I had to hold back my tears.

For several days after that I refused to speak French. But gradually, I realized that I could have handled the situation differently. I could have laughed at myself along with the waiter. I made up my mind to listen carefully to the way French people speak and to try to imitate their accent. I began to speak French again, and I didn't let people's comments about my accent bother me.

I realize now that the waiter was very rude to laugh at me, but I also realize that he did me a favor. Today I speak fluent French with a very good accent. If that waiter hadn't criticized me, I probably wouldn't have improved as much as I did.

C **Work** with a partner. Answer the questions.

1. Where and when did the story take place?

2. Who criticized the writer? What did she do or say? Was the criticism constructive or negative?

3. How did the writer feel?

4. How did the writer respond?

5. What could the writer have done differently?

6. How did the writer change, or what did she learn, as a result of the criticism?

D **Plan** a story about a time when someone criticized you, either constructively or negatively. Outline the story on your own paper. Include answers to questions similar to those in Exercise 1C in your outline.

2 Write

Write the story about the time when someone criticized you, how you responded, and what you learned from the experience. Use Exercises 1A, 1B, and 1C to help you.

3 After you write

A **Check** your writing.

	Yes	No
1. I wrote about who criticized me, where it happened, when it happened, and what the person said.	☐	☐
2. I described how I felt and how I responded.	☐	☐
3. I used past modals or the past unreal conditional to talk about what I should have done differently.	☐	☐
4. I wrote about what I learned or how I changed as a result of the criticism.	☐	☐

B **Share** your writing with a partner.

1. Take turns. Read your partner's story.

2. Comment on your partner's writing. Ask your partner a question. Tell your partner one thing you learned.

UNIT 9 THE RIGHT ATTITUDE

Lesson A Get ready

1 Talk about the pictures

A What does it mean to have a positive or a negative attitude? Give examples.

B Do you think the people in the photos have a positive or a negative attitude? Why do you think so?

2 Listening

A **Listen** and answer the questions.

CD2, Track 11

1. Who is the speaker in this talk? Who are the listeners? Why are they there?

2. Which behaviors can show whether a person has a positive or a negative attitude?

B **Listen again.** Take notes on the key information.

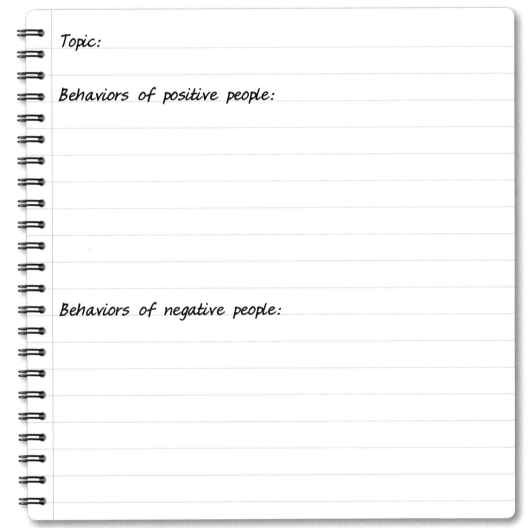

Topic:

Behaviors of positive people:

Behaviors of negative people:

Listen again. Check your notes. Did you miss anything important?

C **Discuss.** Talk with your classmates.

1. Describe some positive and negative people you know. How do they behave?

2. What causes some people to have a negative attitude?

3. What can a person do to change a negative attitude?

Listen for and describe people with positive and negative attitudes **UNIT 9** **83**

Lesson B Adverb clauses of concession

1 Grammar focus: *although* and *even though*

Adverb clauses with *although* and *even though* are called concession clauses. These words signal that the information in the main clause is surprising or unexpected. The dependent clause can go at the beginning or at the end of the sentence. A comma is used if it is at the beginning.

Although Beth is usually a positive person, she sometimes complains about her job.	**Even though** your courses are stressful sometimes, try to have a positive attitude.
Beth sometimes complains about her job **although** she is a positive person.	Try to have a positive attitude **even though** your courses are stressful sometimes.

Watch

2 Practice

A Write. Choose the best clause to complete each sentence. Then write the sentence. Insert a comma if necessary.

1. Mike has a great job.

   a. he complains about his work all the time   b. he really likes his boss

   Although _Mike has a great job, he complains about his work all the time._

2. Susan still feels stressed out.

   a. she goes to stress reduction classes   b. she is starting to feel better

   _____ even though _____

3. John is a positive example for his staff.

   a. some people still complain about him   b. everyone works hard

   Although _____

4. Sam's teacher helped him a lot.

   a. Sam bought his teacher a gift   b. Sam decided to transfer to another class

   Even though _____

5. Jim doesn't like his job.

   a. he stays because of the salary   b. his boss is very critical

   Although _____

6. Peter got an A on the final exam.

   a. he decided to drop the class   b. the accounting class was very hard

   _____ even though _____

B **Talk** with a partner. Compare Ms. Muse with Mr. Grimes. Use *although* or *even though* and the cues provided.

Although Ms. Muse has a stressful job, she always has a smile on her face.

Although Mr. Grimes has an easy job, he never smiles at anybody.

1. has a stressful job /
   always has a smile on her face

2. always helps other people /
   has too much work

3. has a low salary / doesn't complain

4. is never late / lives far away

5. has a sick mother /
   never misses a day of work

6. has an easy job /
   never smiles at anybody

7. never helps others /
   has lots of time

8. has a good salary / says it's not enough

9. is often late / lives near the office

10. has no family responsibilities /
    is often absent from work

Write sentences about Ms. Muse and Mr. Grimes. Use *although* or *even though*.

Although Ms. Muse has a stressful job, she always has a smile on her face.

Ms. Muse always has a smile on her face although she has a stressful job.

③ Communicate

A **Work** in a small group. Choose one or more statements, and complete them with information about your life.

1. Our teacher is usually cheerful although . . .

2. Although I am happy to be in this country, . . .

3. _____ lost his/her job even though . . .

4. I have a good attitude at work/school even though . . .

5. Although I've only been in the United States for a short time, . . .

B **Share** information about your classmates.

1 Before you read

Talk with your classmates. Answer the questions.

1. When you are sick, what do you do to try to recover as quickly as possible?
2. How can having a positive attitude help someone who is sick?

2 Read

Read the story. Listen and read again.

🔊 CD2, Track 12

The Power of Positive Thinking

HUGO ABITBOL came to the United States from Morocco 12 years ago. He went to college, found a job, got married, and had a son. His life was happy and normal in every way – until one day five years ago, when his idyllic world was turned upside down.

On that day, Hugo learned he had invasive prostate cancer. Although he was still a young man, he needed immediate surgery to save his life. He had the operation and spent two months recovering. Now, five years later, he is working and enjoying life as much as ever, even though he knows that the cancer could return any time.

"When life gives you a setback, you can't surrender. You can't give up. You have to persevere, although it's not always easy to keep going," Hugo said.

Hugo is sure it was his positive attitude that helped him overcome the cancer. It wasn't easy. At first, his family was stunned and upset. Hugo told them that they would deal with the challenges of his illness one day at a time.

"You can't stop living just because you have problems," Hugo said. "Even though life can be discouraging, you need to keep moving forward."

Following his surgery, Hugo took several positive steps to speed up his recovery. He joined a support group for cancer survivors. Connecting with other people reminded him that he was not alone and helped him deal with his anxiety about the future.

Also, he was determined to get back to his job managing a garden supply business. Hugo had always adored plants, and he enjoyed interacting with the customers. Having a job he loved helped him stay focused throughout his recovery.

Today, in addition to his job, Hugo volunteers with charities around Miami to help raise awareness about cancer. "I believe if you have the right attitude," he said, "positive things will happen. I count my blessings every day. I know I'm lucky to be here."

3 **After you read**

A **Check** your understanding.

   1. What illness did Hugo have?

   2. What did he do to overcome it?

   3. What is Hugo doing today?

B **Build** your vocabulary.

   1. Look for the words and phrases from the chart in the reading and underline them. Decide if the words are positive or negative. Fill in the clues that helped you guess.

Word	Positive	Negative	Clues
1. idyllic	✓		*happy, normal*
2. invasive			
3. setback			
4. persevere			
5. stunned			
6. anxiety			
7. determined			
8. adored			
9. focused			
10. count one's blessings			

   2. Work with your classmates. Write four more words or phrases from the story that have a positive or negative meaning. Write *P* next to positive words. Write *N* next to negative words.

   a. _____

   b. _____

   c. _____

   d. _____

C **Summarize** the reading. Work with a partner and take turns restating the main points. Try to use vocabulary from Exercise B. Include the following:

   1. Hugo's life before his illness

   2. his operation

   3. the steps in his recovery

   4. the role of positive thinking

   5. Hugo's life today

Determine the central idea of a text and how it is conveyed through key details; identify context clues to determine whether words carry a positive or negative meaning; summarize a text

Lesson D Reading

1 Before you read

Talk with your classmates. Answer the questions.

1. Read the title. What does the suffix *-itis* mean? Can you guess the meaning of *negativitis*?

2. Have you ever worked or studied with a negative person? How did this person's attitude affect you?

2 Read

Read the article. Listen and read again.

CD2, Track 13

Say No to Negativitis

Meet Nelly. Even though she is healthy, does well in her night-school classes, and has a good job, Nelly finds something to complain about in almost every situation. It's a beautiful spring day? "All those flowers make me sneeze." She gets an A minus on a difficult homework assignment? "I should have gotten an A." She gets a pay increase at work? "It's only $20 a week. Big deal."

We all know people like Nelly. Critical, unsmiling, and gloomy, such people seem to have a disease that prevents them from seeing the bright side of life. Some psychologists even have a name for their negative attitude – "negativitis."

The causes of negativitis can be complex. Some people have a negative attitude because of difficulties in their childhood or personal lives. In other people, negativity is a response to unfair treatment. At work, for example, negativitis can develop from employees feeling that they are underpaid or overworked, that their successes are not recognized, or that they are not included in decision making.

Just one person's negative attitude can be enough to contaminate the atmosphere of an entire office or group. Workplaces infected with negativitis show increases in absenteeism, accidents, employee mistakes, and theft. Unless managers recognize employee negativity and take steps to eradicate it, it can lead to major financial losses.

Although management should take an active role in solving the problem of workplace negativity, you, as an employee, can also take steps to combat the toxic effects of negativitis in your workplace or group:

1. Whenever possible, avoid negative, complaining co-workers.

2. Control your own negative comments and negative thinking. *Choose* to think and speak positively.

3. Don't participate in office gossip.

4. Make a list of all the negative words you hear other people using. Remove those words from your vocabulary.

5. Notice and acknowledge other people's good work. Be generous with compliments.

6. Keep the lines of communication open with your boss and co-workers. Seek positive solutions to problems.

3 **After you read**

A **Check** your understanding.

1. The writer uses the words *contaminate*, *infect*, and *toxic* to compare a negative attitude to what?

2. What are some causes of negativitis?

3. What are the consequences of negativitis in the workplace?

4. Name three things that employees can do to combat negativitis at work.

5. Do you think negativitis is really a disease? Why or why not?

B **Build** your vocabulary.

1. Look for the words in the reading that end with the suffixes in the chart and underline them. Fill in each word's part of speech and its meaning. If necessary, use a dictionary to check your answers.

Suffix	Example in reading	Part of speech	Meaning
1. -itis	*negativitis*	*noun*	*illness of negative thinking*
2. -ity			
3. -ist			
4. -ism			
5. -hood			
6. -ate			

2. Work with a partner. Make a list of other words you know that end with the suffixes in the chart. Share your list with your classmates.

_____   _____   _____

_____   _____   _____

C **Summarize** the reading. Close your books. Work with a partner and take turns restating the main points. Then work with a partner to write the summary. Try to use the words in Exercise B. Include the following:

1. definition of negativitis
2. characteristics of negative people
3. causes and effects of negativitis
4. the role of management
5. what employees can do

**For additional development of College and Career Readiness skills, see "The Problem with Optimism,"
a related reading and activities on pages 126–128.**

Cite textual evidence that supports an author's point of view; identify suffixes to
determine part of speech and define meaning; summarize a text

Lesson E Writing

1 Before you write

A **Talk** with a partner. Answer the questions.

1. In the United States, students are usually required to write an essay as part of a college application. What kinds of questions do you think students have to answer for such an essay?

2. Have you ever read or written a college admissions essay? If so, what was it about?

B **Read** Jane's college admissions essay to the University of South Florida. Underline all the positive statements she makes about herself and the school.

University of South Florida – Application (continued)

Question: Please tell us about yourself and your career goals for the future. Why would you like to attend the University of South Florida?

    I am a senior at West Palms High School in Tampa, Florida. In May I will graduate from my high school with honors, and from there I plan to pursue my lifelong dream of becoming a marine biologist.

    I have lived in Florida all my life and have been interested in marine life since I was a child. I attended summer camps with a focus on marine biology and enjoyed every aspect of learning about ocean life. Although I am interested in both plants and animals, I would like to focus on studying animal life in the ocean.

    In preparation for college, I took every biology course offered by my high school, including two advanced marine biology courses in my junior and senior years. I got A's in all my science courses and I am finishing high school with an overall GPA of 3.9.

    The University of South Florida is the perfect school for me because of its excellent program in marine biology. I looked over your course catalog and was impressed by the diverse class offerings you have in this department. The reputation of the program is well known. Additionally, your location close to the Gulf of Mexico is ideal for studying marine life. Finally, I am especially looking forward to taking classes with Dr. Kelly Spires, who wrote the textbooks for my marine biology classes in high school.

    For all of these reasons, I am very interested in attending the University of South Florida. Because of my strong interest in marine biology and the work I have already done in this area, I believe that I am a strong candidate for your program.

C **Plan** your answer to the same college admissions essay question that Jane answered. Take notes in the chart.

Name of the college or university you would like to attend: _____

Questions	Your notes
Paragraph 1: Your background and goals · Where you are from? · Where did you attend high school? · What are your interests? · What would you like to study? · What career would you like to have in the future? Why?	
Paragraph 2: Your preparation · What have you already done (courses, programs, travel, jobs) to prepare for your goal or career?	
Paragraph 3: Reasons for choosing this school	
Paragraph 4: Closing statement · Repeat your interest in the school · Make a positive closing statement about yourself	

2 Write

Write an answer to the question. Use Exercises 1B and 1C to help you.

3 After you write

A **Check** your writing.

	Yes	No
1. I wrote about my background.	☐	☐
2. I wrote about my career goals for the future.	☐	☐
3. I explained why I want to attend this college or university.	☐	☐
4. I ended with a positive statement about myself.	☐	☐

B **Share** your writing with a partner.

1. Take turns. Read your writing to a partner.

2. Comment on your partner's writing. Ask your partner questions. Tell your partner one thing you learned.

Lesson A Get ready

1 Talk about the pictures

A What kinds of things do people write at work? At school?

B What do you think the people in the photos are typing or writing? Why do you think so?

2 Listening

A Listen and answer the questions.

1. Why are writing skills important, according to the lecture?

2. What are some of the findings in the report of the National commission on Writing for America's Families, Schools, and Colleges?

3. What can you do to improve your writing, according to the lecture?

◀)) CD2, Track 14

B Listen again. Take notes on the key information.

◀)) CD2, Track 14

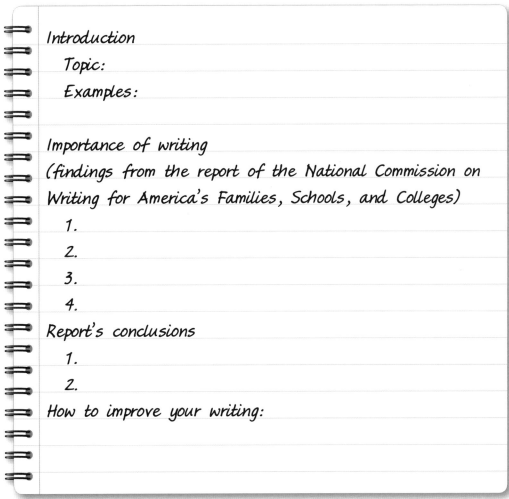

> Introduction
>   Topic:
>   Examples:
>
> Importance of writing
> (findings from the report of the National Commission on
> Writing for America's Families, Schools, and Colleges)
>   1.
>   2.
>   3.
>   4.
> Report's conclusions
>   1.
>   2.
> How to improve your writing:

Listen again. Check your answers. Did you miss anything important?

C Discuss. Talk with your classmates.

1. According to the lecture, writing should be clear, accurate, and concise. What do these words mean?

2. What types of writing do you need to do now? How might this change in the future?

3. Do you have a goal for improving your writing skills? If so, how do you plan to achieve it?

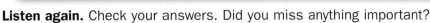

Lesson B Causative verbs

1 Grammar focus: *make*, *have*, and *get*

The causative verbs *make*, *have*, and *get* can mean that one person forces, asks, or persuades another person to do something. In causative sentences, the second verb does not change in tense or number.

Example	Form	Meaning
Mrs. Ovid made her son mow the lawn and walk the dog.	*make* + object + verb	Mrs. Ovid required him to do the chores. He had no choice.
Mrs. Ovid had a handyman fix the broken window.	*have* + object + verb	Mrs. Ovid asked (or paid) the handyman to do a service for her.
Mrs. Ovid got her neighbor to walk the dog while she was away.	*get* + object + *to* + verb	Mrs. Ovid persuaded her neighbor to do a favor for her.

Watch

2 Practice

A **Write.** Rewrite the sentences using *make*, *have*, or *get*.

1. Mrs. Ramsey asked her daughter to answer the phone.

   Mrs. Ramsey had her daughter answer the phone.

2. The boss required everyone to come in early.

   _____

3. Corina paid a manicurist to give her a manicure.

   _____

4. Ajay persuaded a classmate to proofread his history paper.

   _____

5. The school required all the parents to sign a consent form before the children's field trip.

   _____

6. Katarina persuaded all her friends to read her blog.

   _____

7. The school paid a gardener to plant flowers in front of the building.

   _____

8. The city asked a famous artist to paint a mural on the new bridge.

   _____

B **Talk** with a partner. Dr. Brown is the principal of Hamilton High School. Make sentences about her activities.

> Dr. Brown made a student stay after school.

Dr. Brown		
make	**have**	**get**
1. a student / stay after school	4. the janitor / repair a broken window	7. some students / come to school on Saturday to paint over graffiti
2. teachers / come to an important meeting during their lunch hour	5. her assistant / water the plants in her office	8. the parents' association / raise money for a new gym floor
3. her assistant / retype a memo	6. some honor students / show visitors around the campus	9. the mayor / visit the school

Write sentences about Dr. Brown. Use *make*, *have*, or *get*.

Dr. Brown made a student stay after school.

3 Communicate

A **Take** notes on things that one person made, had, or got another person to do. Include your co-workers, classmates, friends, or family members in your notes.

Make	**Have**	**Get**
teacher / me / rewrite my essay	I / former boss / write me a letter of recommendation	My sister / me / babysit for her children

B **Work** with a partner. Make true sentences using your notes. Respond to your partner's sentences.

A My teacher made me rewrite my essay

B Why?

A I made a lot of careless mistakes.

A I had my former boss write me a letter of recommendation.

B Did you have to wait a long time?

A No, just a few days.

A My sister got me to babysit for her children.

B Did you mind?

A No, she babysits for my children sometimes, too.

C **Share** information about your partner with the class.

1 Before you read

Talk with your classmates. Answer the questions.

1. What is *etiquette*? Give examples.

2. Do you think email is a good way to communicate with friends and family? Why or why not?

2 Read

Read the article. Listen and read again.

Email Etiquette 101

🔊 CD2, Track 15

The use of electronic communication has exploded throughout the world in the last decade. In the United States, recent studies have shown that 92 percent of all Internet users communicate via email.

Innovative forms of electronic communication, such as text messaging and "tweeting" (sending short messages of less than 140 characters), are becoming more popular among teens and other computer-savvy people. However, most electronic communication at work and at school still revolves around email messages.

Unfortunately, while many classes and seminars focus on correct ways to write a report or business letter, few, if any, stress the importance of using proper email etiquette. To avoid miscommunication and angry responses, follow these rules:

Composing email

Be sure to clearly say what the message is about in the subject line. If the subject in your subject line is too vague, your email may not even be read.

With bosses, instructors, and new business contacts, keep email formal until you are told that using first names is OK. Keep your email brief and make the tone friendly and respectful. Remember to use good manners, like saying "please" and "thank you."

Don't type in all capital or in all lowercase letters. The first way may make it look like you are shouting, and the second may suggest that you are lazy.

Remember that email messages are not private and that they can be seen by other people. Never fight or gossip in an email message at work.

Sending and forwarding email

Wait to enter the address until after you write the email. That way, you will be more likely to complete the message before sending it. Take time to proofread both the message and the address. Refrain from using the "Reply all" feature unless you are sure everyone on the list needs to read it.

Responding to email in a timely manner is essential. Even if you can't reply right away, send a response saying you received the message and will respond more fully later.

If you want to send a large attachment with an email, ask first. If an attachment is too large, it may not be delivered. It may be best to break up a large attachment into a few smaller ones and to attach them to several different emails.

When it comes to forwarding email, always add a comment to the forwarded message to tell why you are forwarding it and to identify yourself. And remember, do not send personal email from your workplace.

3 After you read

A   Check your understanding.

1. Name three rules to follow when composing an email.

2. Name three rules to follow when sending an email.

3. Why do you think proper email etiquette is important? Can you think of any rules that the article left out? What are they?

B   Build your vocabulary.

1. Look for the words from the chart in the reading and underline them.

2. Write a definition or synonym for each word. Then write an antonym, a word with the opposite meaning. Use a dictionary or thesaurus if necessary.

Word	Synonym	Antonym
1. innovative	*new, modern*	*old-fashioned*
2. savvy		
3. proper		
4. vague		
5. respectful		
6. private		
7. timely		

3. Work in a small group. Read the sentences with the words in the reading. Then use the antonyms to write related sentences with the opposite meaning. For example:

Sentence from the reading: "Innovative forms of electronic communication, such as text messaging and 'tweeting' . . . are becoming more popular . . ."

Your sentence: *These days, handwritten letters are an old-fashioned method of communication.*

C   Summarize the reading. Work with a partner and take turns restating the main points. Then work together to write a summary. Try to use the vocabulary in Exercise B. Include the following topics:

1. importance of email etiquette

2. etiquette for composing an email

3. etiquette for sending and forwarding an email

1 Before you read

Talk with your classmates. Answer the questions.

1. Look at the title of the reading. What do you think it means?

2. Do you think business writing differs from writing for school? How?

2 Read

Read the article. Listen and read again.

CD2, Track 16

Good Business Writing Doesn't Beat Around the Bush

The daily workplace is filled with writing of all sorts, lengths, and purposes, generated by both workers and management. Emails, letters, memos, and reports are regularly distributed and read to keep information flowing smoothly.

The workplace is also filled with lots to read from the outside world. Newspapers, journals, news releases, and documents of all kinds are required reading for businesspeople who want to stay informed and on top of new developments.

But because time is short, businesspeople often just skim or only partially read things in order to extract the information they need. Therefore, it's key for business writing to be clear, crisp, and to the point.

All forms of effective writing in the workplace share several common qualities:

The K.I.S.S. Technique

First and foremost, good business writing uses the K.I.S.S. technique, meaning Keep It Short and Simple. The idea is to convey information in simple, well-organized, and easy-to-read terms. You can avoid confusion by using short sentences when possible and keeping the language simple and familiar. This aids the comprehension of readers who may not have time to read the material in depth.

Directness

Good business writing doesn't beat around the bush, but instead is direct, specific, and to the point. Fuzzy, abstract phrases, such as "a nice person" or "a good idea," force readers to slow down and guess at their real meaning. Concrete, descriptive phrases, such as "a generous young woman" or "an innovative suggestion," enable readers to form clearer images in their minds.

The Active Voice

The passive voice can sometimes confuse readers because it does not say who the performer of an action is. In business writing, it is especially important to be clear about exactly who is doing what.

Thus, instead of saying "Arrangements were made to ship your order immediately," you can write "I made arrangements to ship your order immediately." Instead of "Your complaint is being investigated," write "I am having my assistant investigate your complaint." The active voice not only tells the reader who is responsible for performing the action, it is also more interesting and attention grabbing.

③ **After you read**

A **Check** your understanding.

1. Why is it important to keep business writing short and simple?

2. What is the K.I.S.S. technique?

3. Name two ways that using the active voice can make writing more effective.

B **Build** your vocabulary.

1. Look for the words from the chart in the reading and underline them. Write the meaning from the article.

2. Use a dictionary and write a different meaning for each word.

Word	Meaning in article	Other meaning
1. on top of (prep.)	*informed about*	*at the highest point*
2. short (adj.)		
3. skim (v.)		
4. key (adj.)		
5. crisp (adj.)		
6. fuzzy (adj.)		
7. concrete (adj.)		

3. Work with a partner. Write sentences using the other meaning of the words in the chart.

We had another hiker take a picture of us on top of the mountain.

C **Summarize** the reading. Work with a partner and take turns restating the main points. Then work together to write a summary. Try to use the vocabulary from Exercise B. Include the following topics:

1. key characteristics of business writing

2. the K.I.S.S. technique

3. directness in writing

4. using the active voice

For additional development of College and Career Readiness skills, see "The Limits of Email," a related reading and activities on pages 129–131.

Lesson E Writing

1 Before you write

A **Talk** with your classmates. Answer the questions.

1. What types of reports are written at work? Give examples.

2. Have you ever heard the term "action plan"? Can you guess the purpose of this kind of report?

B **Read** the action plan written by the Office of Student Affairs at a college.

CITY COLLEGE

Office of Student Affairs

Cell-phone Cheating

A growing problem on our campus is students' use of cell phones to cheat on exams. The number of students caught cheating this way increased by more than 15 percent in the past year. The cheating takes several forms:

1. Students send text messages with the answers to test questions to other students in the room.

2. Students photograph test items or test pages and send them to students outside the class.

This cheating has serious consequences for our college. First, students who do not cheat are forced to compete unfairly against those who do. Second, instructors who wish to prevent cheating must spend time and resources creating alternative versions of tests. Third, news about cheating on campus damages the reputation of the college in the community.

To prevent cell-phone cheating, the Office of Student Affairs recommends the following new procedures:

1. Upon entering the exam room, students carrying cell phones must turn them off and leave them with the exam proctor at the front of the room.

2. Students will not be allowed to carry backpacks or heavy jackets to their seats.

3. For classes of 25 or more students, the college will hire additional proctors to supervise exams.

4. Students caught cheating will receive an automatic score of zero on the exam, and they will be required to attend a disciplinary meeting with the Dean of Students.

A notice regarding these new regulations will appear in the college newspaper next Friday, April 20, and it will continue to appear twice a week for the next month. Implementation of the new procedures will begin during spring semester final exams, which will take place May 20–27.

C **Talk** with a partner. Identify and summarize the following parts of the action plan in the model:

1. the problem

2. the consequences of the problem

3. recommendations for solving the problem

4. a schedule for implementing the solutions

D **Plan** an action plan in response to a problem in your class, school, job, or personal life. Use the diagram to organize your writing. Share your diagram with a partner.

Problem: _____

Consequence(s)	**Recommendation(s)**	**Schedule**
1. _____	1. _____	Apr. 20: _____
2. _____	2. _____	Apr. 20–May 20: _____
3. _____	3. _____	May 20–27: _____
	4. _____	

2 Write

Write the action plan. Include the problem, consequence(s), recommendation(s), and time line. Use Exercises 1C and 1D to help you.

3 After you write

A **Check** your writing.

	Yes	No
1. The introductory paragraph introduces and describes the problem.	☐	☐
2. I made recommendations for solving the problem.	☐	☐
3. I suggested a time line for solving the problem.	☐	☐

B **Share** your writing with a partner.

1. Take turns. Read your action plan to a partner.

2. Comment on your partner's writing. Ask your partner questions. Tell your partner one thing you learned.

Before you read, look at the title and think about what you already know about the topic.

Problems with Goal Setting

Setting goals can be motivating and lead to personal success. However, as Ray Williams summarized in his online article "Why Goal Setting Doesn't Work," there are also several potential problems with goal setting.

One area of potential problems is with "stretch goals" — goals that are so challenging that they extend the goal-setter to the limit all at once rather than in incremental steps. In business and industry, an employee who focuses on his goal may neglect other work that is unrelated to the goal; that other work can then become the responsibility of co-workers. For example, a team leader who has to prepare a presentation for the manager neglects her other responsibilities, such as ordering supplies. Co-workers become resentful because they have to cover for her. For individuals, there is also a danger with stretch goals. Often stated in terms of the ideal, goal-setters who don't reach their goals may feel they are failures. For example, a student whose goal is to get straight As gets one B. Rather than recognizing what he has achieved, he focuses on what he didn't achieve.

A goal combined with other work can impact the quality of one's work and one's life. When we set goals, we need to think about the other work that will be happening at the same time. Even if both the new goal and the other work can be completed, each might take longer than projected. The quality of each might also be diminished; that is, outstanding work may become mediocre work. Even if other work doesn't suffer, the effort to complete goals could eventually disrupt a person's work-life balance;

home life and personal enrichment outside of work could be negatively impacted.

Ethical issues can also occur as a result of goal setting, especially when set by others. Say, for example, that an employer gives its repair staff a targeted amount of money to generate within a specific time period. The repair staff may overcharge or perform unnecessary repairs. This was the case in the 1990s when Sears established a quota for its auto repair staff. Unethical behavior can also occur even when people set their own goals if they are required to self-report. Experiments conducted by Schweitzer and Ordonez have shown that in these cases many people who haven't achieved their goals will lie in the self-report.

Yet another problem with goals is the danger of spending more time making them than trying to achieve them. Setting goal after goal and constantly reevaluating them is time-consuming. While it might be worthwhile to reevaluate a goal, the time it takes to create and manage a goal shouldn't overshadow the fact that it needs to be completed. In situations like this, goal setting can actually become a waste of time and an excuse for procrastination.

In summary, goal setting can be detrimental rather than beneficial for several reasons. First, stretch goals at work can result in co-worker resentment; and for individuals, the stretch goal can lead to failure. Additionally, too much focus on goals can upset the work-life balance, and constant reevaluation can deflect from achievement. Finally, the desire to achieve a goal can lead to unethical behavior.

UNIT 1

1 Check your understanding

1. What four potential problems with goal setting does the author of *Problems with Goal Setting* discuss?
2. According to the article, why do co-workers get upset when a team leader fulfills one goal and neglects others?
3. What example does the author provide to show how quality of work can be affected by goal setting?
4. Explain in your own words how work-life balance can be impacted by goal setting.
5. In the fifth paragraph, what word does the author use to mean *valuable*?
6. The article describes an experiment conducted on people who self-report on their goals. Describe in your own words the unethical behavior that the results revealed.

2 Build your vocabulary

A Find these words in the paragraph indicated and underline them. Which words are positive in this context? Which words are negative? What clues helped you guess?

Word	Positive	Negative	Clue
1. motivating, ¶1	✔		. . . lead to personal success
2. incremental, ¶2			
3. resentful, ¶2			
4. mediocre, ¶3			
5. failure, ¶2			
6. time-consuming, ¶5			
7. detrimental, ¶6			

B Find each of the following academic words in the article and underline the sentence.

> achieve   challenging   constantly   diminished   ethical   goal

Then, on another piece of paper, copy and complete the chart.

Academic word	Phrase or sentence from article	Part of speech	Dictionary definition	My sentence
achieve	Yet another problem with goals is the danger of spending more time making them than trying to achieve them.	verb	to reach or acquire	The student achieved her dream of attending college.

3 Talk with a partner

Answer each question with evidence from the reading. Use one of the phrases in the Useful Language box.

1. How can goal setting be detrimental? Give an example.
2. What might cause resentment in the workplace?
3. How might goal setting promote unethical behavior?

USEFUL LANGUAGE
Phrases to report someone else's ideas:
_____ indicated that . . .
_____ observed that . . .

Ventures
2ⁿᵈ Edition
STUDENT'S BOOK **TRANSITIONS**

> **Objective: CCR Anchor 9:** Analyze how two or more texts address similar themes or topics in order to build knowledge or to compare the approaches the authors take.

4 Analyze the texts

Review the following texts to answer the questions below: (1) Student Book, p. 6, *Setting Goals for the Future;* (2) Student Book, p. 8, *Keys for Success at Work;* (3) Extended Reading, *Problems with Goal Setting.*

1. According to the text *Setting Goals for the Future,* how does the author define setting goals?
2. In the same text, the author gives several important points to consider when setting goals. Identify three and give examples from the text to support your choices.
3. What does the author of *Keys for Success at Work* suggest people do if they are not strong in the skills and qualities he lists?
4. How does the author of *Problems with Goal Setting* define "stretch goals"? Restate the definition in your own words. Which point in the article *Setting Goals for the Future* would prevent this problem?

5 Before you write

Is goal setting more beneficial or detrimental to achieving success? Use the information from Exercises 1–4 and evidence from the three texts to support your opinion. Complete the graphic organizer with your opinion, three key arguments, and evidence to support each argument. Add a conclusion.

Opinion:	
Three Key Arguments	**Evidence to Support Arguments**
1.	1.
2.	2.
3.	3.
Conclusion:	

6 Write

Is goal setting more beneficial or detrimental to achieving success? What is your opinion? Use your graphic organizer and evidence from the three texts to support your opinion.

7 After you write

A Check your writing. Did you include all the ideas in your graphic organizer?

B Share your writing with a partner.

    a. Take turns. Read your writing to your partner.

    b. Read your partner's writing to yourself. Compare it to your partner's graphic organizer.

    c. Comment on your partner's writing: Ask one question; share one thing you learned.

Before reading the entire article, skim each paragraph to identify the purpose or focus of that paragraph.

Dangers of Too Much Self-Confidence

A lack of self-confidence, or self-esteem, is generally viewed negatively. Human beings are social creatures. A lack of self-confidence removes opportunities, such as meeting new people or advancing professionally. However, self-confidence is a double-edged sword. Too much self-confidence can be just as problematic.

Some people with an overabundance of self-confidence are convinced that their perspective is better than the perspective of others. This can lead to conflict. Take, for example, a team trying to decide what information to include in a short presentation. One member, confident that everything is relevant to the project, insists everything be included. Although others counter that the time allotted for the presentation is too short to include everything, the overly confident team member stubbornly continues to impose her point of view. Being so confident in this context negates valuable input that others can contribute to the presentation.

Behavior such as that described above can cause another problem with excess self-confidence: poor interpersonal relationships. Overconfidence can result in not listening to other people's opinions, causing others to perceive the person as having a sense of superiority or an over-inflated ego. An outcome of being exposed to such behavior can be that the willingness of colleagues to work with such a person again will diminish dramatically. Moreover, in a work setting, management may avoid promoting employees who exhibit such behavior to higher positions that require working with others regularly.

A tendency to be verbally defensive is another potential behavior of some individuals with too much self-esteem according to a study by Kernis, Lakey, and Heppner. Based on their interviews of 100 undergraduates, they concluded that there is a difference in behavior between those with high self-esteem that is stable and those whose high self-esteem is fragile. When others disagree with someone whose high self-esteem is fragile, the person may become defensive, such as by blaming others or making excuses. If the team in the example given above consents to the dominant person's viewpoint and the presentation is not well received, the self-confident person who is fragile may become overly defensive and accuse other team members for the failed presentation.

Self-confidence is a double-edged sword for several reasons. Similarly, while it is important to be confident, it is equally important to maintain some level of modesty. While it is important to express opinions, it is equally important to listen to others. People will avoid those who believe themselves infallible. They will also avoid those who become defensive when others question their opinions. Overconfidence, as much as a lack of self-confidence, can lead to a solitary lifestyle in both academic and career settings.

1 Check your understanding

1. What are three dangers of too much self-confidence?
2. Why might a person not get promoted to the managerial level? Cite evidence from the text.
3. Explain the study by Kernis, Lakey, and Heppner. Who were the participants in the study? What were the conclusions?
4. According to the author, how can overconfidence affect interpersonal relationships?
5. In the second sentence of the fourth paragraph, who does *they* refer to?

2 Build your vocabulary

A It's important to relate academic words to words you use in everyday conversation. Find and underline each of the following academic words in the paragraphs indicated. Then, in Column 2, write the academic word that best matches the everyday word in Column 1. Write the phrase or sentence from the article in Column 3.

conflict, ¶2   convinced, ¶2   exhibit, ¶3   input, ¶2   lack, ¶1   relevant, ¶2

Everyday word	Academic word	Phrase or sentence from article
1. not enough	*lack*	*A lack of self-confidence*
2. to be sure		
3. disagreement		
4. connected or related		
5. ideas or information		
6. show		

B Find each of the following academic words in the article and underline the sentence.

colleagues   consents   impose   outcome   perceive   potential

Then, on another piece of paper, copy and complete the chart.

Academic word	Phrase or sentence from article	Part of speech	Dictionary definition	My sentence
colleagues	*...that the willingness of colleagues to work with such a person again will diminish dramatically.*	*noun*	*someone you work with*	*My colleagues in the office agreed with the proposal.*

3 Talk with a partner

Answer each question with evidence from the reading. Use one of the phrases in the Useful Language box.

1. In the text, the author gives an example of a stubborn team member who refuses to change his opinion. Use your own words to explain the problem and consequences.
2. What are some ways overconfidence in the workplace can be detrimental?
3. What do people do when they are verbally defensive?

> **USEFUL LANGUAGE**
> Phrases to cite evidence:
> According to the article, . . .
> According to the author, . . .

Objective: CCR Anchor 9: Analyze how two or more texts address similar themes or topics in order to build knowledge or to compare the approaches the authors take.

4 Analyze the texts

Review the following texts to answer the questions below: (1) Student Book, p. 16, *Understanding Self-Confidence;* (2) Student Book, p. 18, *Building Self-Confidence;* (3) Extended reading, *Dangers of Too Much Self-Confidence.*

1. How does the author of *Understanding Self-Confidence* define self-confidence? Restate the definition in your own words.
2. In *Understanding Self-Confidence,* what does the author identify as some behaviors of people who don't have self-confidence?
3. According to the author of *Building Self-Confidence,* there are several strategies to build self-confidence. Identify strategies that can help prevent at least three of the behaviors listed in Question 2.
4. In *Dangers of Too Much Self-Confidence,* the author refers to the *double-edged sword* of self-confidence. Use examples from the text, restated in your own words, to define this term.

5 Before you write

Complete the graphic organizer with the behaviors and consequences of people who do not have self-confidence and those who have too much self-confidence. Use the information from Exercises 1–4 and evidence from the three texts.

TOPIC No self-confidence		TOPIC Too much self-confidence
Behaviors 1. _____ 2. _____	⟷	**Behaviors** 1. _____ 2. _____
Consequences 1. _____ 2. _____	⟷	**Consequences** 1. _____ 2. _____

6 Write

Compare the behaviors and consequences of people who do not have self-confidence with those who have too much self-confidence. Decide which of the two is more problematic. Use the graphic organizer and evidence from the three texts to support your decision.

7 After you write

A Check your writing. Did you include all the ideas in your graphic organizer?

B Share your writing with a partner.

    a. Take turns. Read your writing to your partner.

    b. Read your partner's writing to yourself. Compare it to your partner's graphic organizer.

    c. Comment on your partner's writing: Ask one question; share one thing you learned.

STUDENT'S BOOK TRANSITIONS

Before reading the entire article, read the first paragraph and identify the topic sentence.

Disadvantages of Volunteerism

Volunteerism has been on the upswing recently for both students and potential employees. Many educational institutions – both at the secondary and college level – are encouraging, and some even requiring, volunteerism because of its perceived positive aspects. Many companies are using volunteers to cut costs. Because of this trend, it is important to take a close look at potential pitfalls for both the volunteer and the company.

The Volunteer's Point of View

One complaint of volunteers is that the duties they were recruited for were misrepresented. In other words, there is a mismatch between the volunteer's expectations and the company's expectations. An example is a volunteer at a child-care center who expects his main task to be playing with the children, but finds it to be cleaning up the kitchen after lunch and snack time.

One of the most common complaints of volunteers is that they are being exploited. That is, they don't feel that they are being taught helpful skills; rather, they are assigned "busy" work — petty or insignificant tasks — that they view as a waste of time and as ones that don't require skill. This complaint is especially common in the case of mandatory — required — volunteering.

An example of another common complaint comes from a student who experienced mandatory volunteering while attending community college in Florida. He says it overtaxed his schedule, which impacted his health. He also complained that the volunteering often forced him to neglect his studies in order to complete the mandatory hours. A recently published report also indicates that there is potential for a negative impact on health — both when the volunteer is placed in uncomfortable or difficult circumstances without adequate counseling and when having to work with someone whose personality clashes with their own. Both of these situations can cause anxiety, frustration, and stress. Many studies also indicate that time spent volunteering can result in neglecting other aspects of one's life.

The Company's Point of View

Companies that use volunteers in their workplace need to anticipate potential conflict with their paid staff. Paid staff may fear the company's use of volunteers, thinking it can result in a reduction in their work hours or even job loss. Paid staff may also feel that the volunteers take over.

Equally challenging for companies that use volunteers is the staff time that volunteer programs require for recruitment, training, and supervision. Each of these may be more time-consuming than anticipated; moreover, each has hidden costs in terms of time they take away from regular staff duties.

Some companies shy away from using volunteers in their workplace because of a lack of accountability. They aren't sure how to get rid of volunteers who turn out to be unsuitable, irresponsible, or under-performing. Moreover, they fear that volunteers, because they aren't under contract and don't expect to be paid, may leave unexpectedly. Guidelines that make roles and responsibilities clear can avoid such issues.

Before individuals commit to volunteering, they need to carefully consider their skills, expectations, and schedules. Before companies decide to recruit volunteers, they should consider the impact on paid employees, staff time, and hidden costs.

UNIT 3

1 Check your understanding

1. What are three complaints volunteers have?
2. What are three challenges employers have?
3. In the first paragraph, what trend is the author referring to?
4. What is the mismatch in the example of the child-care worker?
5. Has volunteering increased or decreased lately? What word gives you this information?
6. In the section *The Company's Point of View,* what does "it" in the second sentence refer to?

2 Build your vocabulary

A English often uses punctuation, such as dashes and commas, with synonyms and phrases to signal definitions. Look for the words in the paragraph indicated and complete the chart.

Word	Signal	Definition, explanation or example
1. educational institutions, ¶1	*dashes*	*secondary and college*
2. misrepresented, ¶2		
3. being exploited, ¶3		
4. busy work, ¶3		
5. petty, ¶3		
6. mandatory, ¶3 / 4		

B Find each academic word in the article and underline the sentence.

> adequate   anticipate   aspects   indicate   tasks   trend

Then, on another piece of paper, copy and complete the chart.

Academic word	Phrase or sentence from article	Part of speech	Dictionary definition	My sentence
adequate	*The volunteer is placed in uncomfortable or difficult circumstances without adequate counseling.*	*adjective*	*having enough in quantity*	*Her income isn't adequate to pay her bills.*

3 Talk with a partner

Answer each question with evidence from the reading.
Use one of the phrases in the Useful Language box.

1. What do volunteers complain about?
2. What challenges does volunteering present for companies?
3. Why is it important to consider the potential pitfalls of volunteerism?

> **USEFUL LANGUAGE**
> Phrases to cite evidence:
> The article states that . . .
> The author states that . . .

> **Objective: CCR Anchor 9:** Analyze how two or more texts address similar themes or topics in order to build knowledge or to compare the approaches the authors take.

4 Analyze the texts

Review the following texts to answer the questions below: (1) Student Book, p. 26, *Volunteering the Family Way;* (2) Student Book, p. 28, *Volunteering While at College;* (3) Extended Reading, *Disadvantages of Volunteerism.*

1. According to the text *Volunteering While at College*, there are at least three benefits to volunteering. Identify the strongest benefit. Use evidence from the text to support your choice.
2. In the text *Volunteering the Family Way*, what concern and benefit does Aubrey share about volunteering?
3. The text *Disadvantages of Volunteerism* discusses potential pitfalls for volunteers. Restate two of these pitfalls in your own words.
4. Analyze the volunteer situations discussed in the texts on pages 26 and 28. How might the potential pitfalls identified in Question 3 occur in these volunteer situations?

5 Before you write

Do the benefits of volunteering outweigh the disadvantages? Use the information from Exercises 1–4 and evidence from the three texts to support your opinion. Complete the graphic organizer with your opinion, three key arguments, and evidence to support each argument. Add a concluding sentence.

Opinion:	
Three Key Arguments	**Evidence to Support Arguments**
1.	1.
2.	2.
3.	3.
Conclusion:	

6 Write

Do the benefits of volunteering outweigh the disadvantages? Use the graphic organizer and evidence from the three texts to support your opinion.

7 After you write

A Check your writing. Did you include all the ideas in your graphic organizer?

B Share your writing with a partner.

   a. Take turns. Read your writing to your partner.

   b. Read your partner's writing to yourself. Compare it to your partner's graphic organizer.

   c. Comment on your partner's writing: Ask one question; share one thing you learned.

Before you read the entire article, read the first paragraph to determine who the article is for – employers or potential employees.

Online Job Applications

In recent years, online job applications have become quite common because they streamline the application process. Many employers, such as Walmart – one of the largest employers in the world, accept only online applications because the process is efficient and cost effective for the company. But it is also efficient and cost effective for the applicant. In addition, technology can help the applicant avoid errors. For these reasons, as well as the movement of companies to online applications, applicants need to master the skill of applying for jobs online.

Online job applications are efficient in several ways. Applicants can apply at any time and from any place rather than only during the hours the employer is open. They don't have to stand in line. They also avoid the situation of going to the company and having to make a second trip because the employer has run out of applications. They can send out three or four résumés an hour with the click of a button. Likewise, email is more efficient than other mailing methods because it arrives instantaneously. Applying for jobs online can also be cost effective: it doesn't require paper, it doesn't require envelopes, and it doesn't require postage. Moreover, applicants can complete the form in the comfort of their home and get help completing the application from friends and family members. This is especially important for first-time job applicants.

Another advantage of online applications is their reliance on technology. The technology can help humans avoid errors. For example, applicants can avoid making spelling errors by using spell check and they can avoid accidentally missing sections because the software will alert them if they do. They can also be alerted to what the company is looking for through the use of keywords built into the software. Finally, they will probably receive an automated response letting them know that their application has been received.

On the other hand, online applications can present hurdles for the applicant. Because some companies receive large numbers of applications, they often use software for the initial screening. As a result, large numbers are tossed because answers, such as salary range and credentials, don't match the answers that have been programmed into the software. Furthermore, online applications often have a limitation on the number of characters allowed. Sometimes this makes it very difficult for the applicant to clearly state a response. In addition, an applicant's use of company software on their home computer often leads to technical glitches, causing considerable frustration.

In spite of the disadvantages that online job applications can create, there are two realities that job applicants must face: an increasing number of companies are moving to online applications and competition for jobs is at an all-time high. Therefore, it is important for job applicants to recognize the strengths of online applications and master the skills needed to make it through the screening process.

UNIT 4

1 Check your understanding

1. What is the main idea of the last paragraph? Restate it in your own words.
2. According to the article, what are three advantages of online job applications?
3. According to the article, why are online applications particularly helpful to a person who hasn't completed many applications?
4. Why are so many online applications discarded?
5. In the fourth paragraph, what word or phrase identifies the word *glitches* as positive or negative?
6. What does *this* refer to in the last sentence of the second paragraph?

2 Build your vocabulary

A Transitions are words and phrases that link ideas between sentences and paragraphs as well as within sentences. Some transitions signal addition of ideas – such as *similarly*. Other transitions signal contrast between ideas – such as *however*. Find the following transitions, words and phrases in the paragraph indicated. Identify the two ideas they connect. Then identify the purpose of the transition by checking the correct box.

Transition word	First idea	Second idea	Purpose	
			Addition	Contrast
1. in addition, ¶1	efficient & cost effective for applicant	help applicant avoid errors	✓	
2. likewise, ¶2				
3. moreover, ¶2				
4. on the other hand, ¶4				
5. furthermore, ¶4				
6. in addition, ¶4				
7. in spite of, ¶5				

B Find each of the following academic words in the text and underline the sentence.

> automated   methods   process   range   reliance   sections

Then, on another piece of paper, copy and complete the chart.

Academic word	Phrase or sentence from article	Part of speech	Dictionary definition	My sentence
automated	...they will probably receive an automated response	adjective	operated by machines or computers in order to reduce the work done by humans	I called the school and got an automated message with my teacher's phone number.

3 Talk with a partner

Answer each question with evidence from the article. Use one of the phrases in the Useful Language box.

1. According to the article, how can applying online be cost effective?
2. Give examples from the article of ways that online applications can help applicants avoid making errors.
3. According to the article, how can online applications be difficult for an applicant?

> **USEFUL LANGUAGE**
> Phrases to cite an example:
>
> An example from the article is . . .
> An example the author gave is . . .

> **Objective: CCR Anchor 9:** Analyze how two or more texts address similar themes or topics in order to build knowledge or to compare the approaches the authors take.

4 Analyze the texts

Review the following texts to answer the questions below: (1) Student Book, p. 36, *Beware of Scammers!*; (2) Student Book, p. 38, *Ten Tips for a Great Job Application;* (3) Extended reading, *Online Job Applications.*

1. According to the last three paragraphs of *Beware of Scammers!*, what do job applicants need to be concerned about?
2. Review the disadvantages of online applications in *Online Job Applications* and the problems identified in your response to Question 1. Identify what you think are the two most serious disadvantages from either or both texts. Use evidence to support your choices.
3. *Ten Tips for a Great Job Application* discusses potential problems in applying for jobs. *Online Job Applications* gives solutions for at least two of these problems. Identify the problems and how online applications can resolve them.
4. What can you conclude after reading the last paragraph of *Online Job Applications* and the last paragraph of *Beware of Scammers!*? Restate your conclusion in one sentence.

5 Before you write

Do the advantages of submitting online applications outweigh the disadvantages? Use the information from Exercises 1–4 and evidence from the three texts to support your opinion. Complete the graphic organizer with your three key arguments and evidence to support each argument.

Opinion:	
Three Key Arguments	**Evidence to Support Arguments**
1.	1.
2.	2.
3.	3.
Conclusion:	

6 Write

Do the advantages of submitting online applications outweigh the disadvantages? Use the information in Exercise 4, the graphic organizer, and evidence from the three texts to support your opinion.

7 After you write

A Check your writing. Did you include all the ideas in your graphic organizer?

B Share your writing with a partner.

    a. Take turns. Read your writing to your partner.

    b. Read your partner's writing to yourself. Compare it to your partner's graphic organizer.

    c. Comment on your partner's writing: Ask one question; share one thing you learned.

STUDENT'S BOOK TRANSITIONS

After reading each paragraph, stop and look up. State in your own words both the main idea of that paragraph and the supporting points for the paragraph's main idea.

Accessing "Hidden Jobs"

Most job seekers spend the majority of their search time reviewing job postings and preparing for the job interview. One problem with this approach is that job seekers who rely on job postings miss out on applying for "hidden jobs" – jobs that never get advertised. Some estimate that as much as 80 percent of job vacancies fall into the hidden job category. This means job seekers who depend on job postings are accessing only about 20 percent of the jobs available. Another problem with this approach is that companies that fill hidden jobs learn about the candidates through internal promotions or referrals and recommendations from people who know the candidates.

The message for job seekers is to reapportion the time they spend searching. In his book *The Essential Guide for Hiring and Getting Hired,* Lou Adler advocates a 20 / 20 / 60 rule: 20 percent to review and respond to job postings, 20 percent to build a web presence, and 60 percent to networking. The initial 20 percent is where most job seekers currently devote the majority of their time. They review want ads, file applications, and prepare to be interviewed.

A web presence, advocated in the second 20 percent, is anything online that discusses or represents an individual. It is important for two reasons: it is a way that an employer can find a potential applicant and it provides the employer with information about the potential applicant. According to a survey by Jobvite, 92 percent of employers either use or plan to use social networks for recruiting. This means the employer finds the applicant, rather than the applicant finding the employer! According to a study by OfficeTeam, more than one-third of companies feel that online profiles replace traditional résumés. One way to develop a web presence is to create your own website. Another way is to use existing websites, such as LinkedIn, Facebook, or Twitter.

Networking, the 60 percent portion of the 20 / 20 / 60 rule, is the informal sharing of information among individuals and groups, usually for a common purpose. Individuals seeking a job can use networks to make connections with people working for the company where they are seeking employment. Networking can also help the job seeker learn about hidden jobs and develop relationships with people who can recommend them to employers. According to Adler, the likelihood of being interviewed and hired is 50–100 times greater for candidates who are referred than for candidates who respond to a posted job. Through networking and referrals, companies are able to hire the best candidates. Family, friends, and colleagues are part of one's network. References and individuals employed where one is seeking a job can also be part of a network.

In today's job market, applicants need to utilize the most effective strategies to obtain meaningful employment. These strategies include making the best use of time, trying to maximize visibility, and widening the circle of key supporters. There is a saying, "Always a bridesmaid, never a bride." In seeking jobs, applicants want to avoid being "always interviewed, never hired."

1 Check your understanding

1. In your own words, explain the 20 / 20 / 60 rule that is described in the article.
2. The author refers to a "hidden job category". Explain this category in your own words.
3. According to the article, how do companies find out about potential employees if they don't fill out an application?
4. What are two ways to have a web presence according to the author?
5. In the second paragraph, what word tells you that job applicants should divide their time differently when they are looking for jobs?
6. The fifth sentence of the first paragraph states, "Another problem with this approach is . . ." What does *this approach* refer to?

2 Build your vocabulary

A English uses suffixes to change the part of speech of a word. Find the words that end in the suffixes in the paragraphs indicated. Complete the chart. Use a dictionary if necessary.

Suffix	Example(s) from reading	Part of speech	Root word	Part of speech
1. -al, ¶3 (having the characteristic of) changes noun to adjective	*traditional*	*adjective*	*tradition*	*noun*
2. -ity, ¶1 / 2 (quality of) changes adjective to noun				
3. -ful, ¶5 (full of) changes noun to adjective				
4. -tion, ¶1 (act or process) changes verb to noun				
5. -ize, ¶5 (to become) changes noun to verb				
6. -er, ¶1 / 2 / 4 (one who) changes verb to noun				

B Find each of the following academic words in the article and underline the sentence.

> advocates   networking   obtain   seeking   strategies   utilize

Then, on another piece of paper, copy and complete the chart.

Academic word	Phrase or sentence from article	Part of speech	Dictionary definition	My sentence
advocates	*Lou Adler advocates a 20 / 20 / 60 rule...*	*verb*	*to propose or support an idea*	*The students advocate lower fees for college textbooks.*

3 Talk with a partner

Cite evidence from the reading. Use one of the phrases in the Useful Language box.

1. What does OfficeTeam say about sending résumés online?
2. What are three things Lou Adler recommends to get a job?
3. What does Jobvite's survey tell us?

USEFUL LANGUAGE

Phrases to identify a source:
[Source's name] claims that . . .
[Author's name] recommends that . . .

Ventures
2nd Edition
STUDENT'S BOOK
TRANSITIONS

> **Objective: CCR Anchor 9:** Analyze how two or more texts address similar themes or topics in order to build knowledge or to compare the approaches the authors take.

4 Analyze the texts

Review the following texts to answer the questions below: (1) Student Book, p. 46, *Keys to a Successful Interview!* and (2) Extended reading, *Accessing "Hidden Jobs."*

1. In *Keys to a Successful Interview!*, Carlos and Sheila both apply for a job. Why didn't Carlos and Sheila get hired? What suggestions does the author of *Accessing "Hidden Jobs"* make about what they should do differently next time even before they interview?

2. Sheila takes the time to research the company she is applying to. However, the author of *Accessing "Hidden Jobs"* suggests a job applicant needs to actually make connections with employees. Which part of the 20 / 20 / 60 rule would Sheila be addressing if she had made those connections? What is one benefit for Sheila if she makes these connections next time?

3. The author of *Accessing "Hidden Jobs"* refers to the hidden job market. If Carlos and Sheila are relying only on publicly advertised jobs, what percentage of available jobs are they actually accessing? What does Adler say would greatly increase their chances of being interviewed and hired?

4. In the last paragraph of *Accessing "Hidden Jobs,"* there is a quote about bridesmaids and brides. Restate it in your own words. How does it apply to Carlos's and Sheila's job search opportunities?

5 Before you write

Do you agree or disagree that job applicants such as Carlos and Sheila benefit from implementing the 20 / 20 / 60 rule to gain meaningful employment? If you disagree, what are alternative ways to spend time in order to get hired? Use the information from Exercises 1–4 and evidence from the two texts to support your opinion. Complete the graphic organizer with your three key arguments and evidence to support each argument.

Opinion:	
Three Key Arguments	**Evidence to Support Arguments**
1.	1.
2.	2.
3.	3.
Conclusion:	

6 Write

Do you agree or disagree that job applicants such as Carlos and Sheila benefit from implementing the 20 / 20 / 60 rule to gain meaningful employment? If you disagree, provide alternative ways for job seekers like them to spend their time in order to get hired. Use the graphic organizer and evidence from the three texts to support your opinion.

7 After you write

A Check your writing. Did you include all the ideas in your graphic organizer?

B Share your writing with a partner.

    a. Take turns. Read your writing to your partner.

    b. Read your partner's writing to yourself. Compare it to your partner's graphic organizer.

    c. Comment on your partner's writing: Ask one question; share one thing you learned.

Before you read the entire article, read the first paragraph and determine the focus of the article. Then read the last paragraph and identify the key supporting points.

Making the Best of Small Talk

Small talk is defined by the Merriam-Webster's dictionary as "informal, friendly conversation about unimportant subjects." People use it to initiate conversation or as a greeting and don't expect detailed answers. However, when using small talk, there are several things to consider.

People may have negative reactions to small talk because they consider it superficial or find it intrusive. Many small talk questions – for example, "How's your day going?", "What's new?", or "Nice day, isn't it?" – are somewhat formulaic. Because these kinds of questions are standard, fixed, or unoriginal, people often don't really listen to the responses; they can usually predict the answer. Some people also find small talk intrusive: if they are thinking about something important, the inconsequential, unimportant questions interrupt their thoughts.

Another problem with small talk is that what is appropriate varies from culture to culture. Cultures with more formal rules for communication and a strong emphasis on social hierarchy may consider it inappropriate or rude to engage in casual conversation with superiors. Similarly, some cultures consider it inappropriate to initiate small talk or share personal information with strangers. Different cultures may also have different expectations on how to answer small talk questions. For example, people from some cultures, when asked "How are you?" may begin a detailed description of how they feel and are confused when the questioner walks away. Yet another difference across cultures is whether it is appropriate to share personal opinions. For example, the speaker may say,

"Wasn't that speech last night great?" When others disagree, it puts them in an awkward position; they are uncomfortable expressing a conflicting point of view.

Some level of small talk is an important part of communication in the United States, but because of differences in attitudes among individuals and differences in expectations across cultures, people need to be aware of ways to address issues that might occur. One way to address the negative perceptions of small talk is to use it as an opener but then go beyond it, using strategies that will result in more meaningful exchanges. New acquaintances often use small talk to learn basic facts about each other, but then they can probe deeper with additional questions. For example, they follow up questions such as "What do you do?" with ones like "How long have you been doing that job?" and "What attracted you to that job?". Friends, family members, and old acquaintances can use small talk to catch up when they haven't seen each other for some time. To move beyond the superficial, the questioner can again ask follow-up questions related to the initial response. For the question "What have you been doing lately?", a possible follow-up to the response might be something like "How long have you been doing that?"

In summary, small talk can have negative results. To make the best of it, people who initiate small talk need to be able to judge a person's attitude about it. In addition, they need to be aware of which small talk topics are acceptable and which are taboo in different cultures. Finally, they should be able to adjust their own small talk behavior.

1 Check your understanding

1. According to the article, what should people who initiate small talk consider?
2. Explain in your own words why, in the third paragraph, the author says *the questioner walks away*.
3. According to the author, what can a person do to get beyond superficial questions?
4. What are two questions one can ask for more meaningful exchanges according to the article?
5. In the fourth paragraph, what word means *to go beyond something*?
6. In the third sentence of the second paragraph, what does *these kinds of questions* refer to?

2 Build your vocabulary

A Find the words in Column 1 in the paragraphs indicated and underline them. They are all negative. For each one, identify the clue that tells you it is negative.

Word	Clue
1. superficial, ¶2	. . . *people may have negative reactions*
2. intrusive, ¶2	
3. inconsequential, ¶2	
4. inappropriate, ¶3	
5. awkward, ¶3	
6. taboo, ¶5	

B Find each of the following academic words in the article and underline the sentence.

> adjust   aware   initiate   issues   topics   varies

Then, on another piece of paper, copy and complete the chart.

Academic word	Phrase or sentence from article	Part of speech	Dictionary definition	My sentence
adjust	*. . .adjust their own small talk behavior*	*verb*	*to change something slightly to make it fit or work better*	*We all need time to adjust to a new situation.*

3 Talk with a partner

Answer each question with evidence from the reading. Use one of the phrases in the Useful Language box.

1. According to the article, what are two reasons small talk can be problematic?
2. In the article, the author describes a situation where a person asked a question and when the person answered, the questioner walked away. Why did that happen?
3. Why is it important to consider the culture of a person before making small talk?

> **USEFUL LANGUAGE**
> Phrases to cite evidence:
> The author states that . . .
> The article points out that . . .

Objective: CCR Anchor 9: Analyze how two or more texts address similar themes or topics in order to build knowledge or to compare the approaches the authors take.

4 Analyze the texts

Review the following texts to answer the questions below: (1) Student Book, p. 56, *Small Talk, Big Problems;* (2) Student Book, p. 58, *Strategies for Successful Small Talk;* (3) Extended Reading, *Making the Best of Small Talk.*

1. In *Strategies for Successful Small Talk*, strategy #7 explains one way people in the United States use small talk. Where can you find a similar way of using small talk in *Making the Best of Small Talk*?
2. In *Small Talk, Big Problems,* the author provides information about polite ways to close a conversation. Locate additional closing statements in *Strategies for Successful Small Talk.*
3. In *Small Talk, Big Problems*, Miguel is confused about some conversations with his co-workers. According to *Making the Best of Small Talk*, why is Miguel confused?
4. All three texts provide suggestions for how to deal with small talk issues. Provide one suggestion from each of the three texts.

5 Before you write

In today's diverse workforce with many employees like Miguel, do the identified problems suggest small talk should be used more carefully? Why or why not? Use the information from Exercises 1–4 and evidence from the three texts to complete the graphic organizer.

Opinion:	
Three Key Arguments	**Evidence to Support Arguments**
1.	1.
2.	2.
3.	3.
Conclusion:	

6 Write

In today's diverse workforce with many employees like Miguel, do the identified problems suggest small talk should be used more carefully? Why or why not? Use the graphic organizer and evidence from the three texts to support your opinion.

7 After you write

A Check your writing. Did you include all the ideas in your graphic organizer?

B Share your writing with a partner.

   a. Take turns. Read your writing to your partner.
   b. Read your partner's writing to yourself. Compare it to your partner's graphic organizer.
   c. Comment on your partner's writing: Ask one question; share one thing you learned.

Reading Tip: Before reading the entire article, read the title, the first paragraph, and the first sentence in the other paragraphs to identify who the advice is for.

Strategies for Dealing with Bad Behavior

Bad behavior is measured by the impact it has on others. Bad behaviors and attitudes are like viruses – they can spread from the carrier to those around them. Whether from a classmate, a co-worker, or a manager, stopping bad behavior before it spreads is crucial to the health of the group.

Individuals need strategies for dealing with friends or colleagues who have annoying habits, gossip, or have bad tempers. In order to change these behaviors, the first step is to help the person become aware of the behavior and its impact on others. After the awareness step, employ different strategies for different behaviors. In response to annoying habits, start with the impact of the behavior rather than on the behavior itself. For example, if someone is speaking in a loud voice, don't say, "Your voice is too loud." Rather, say, "It's difficult to concentrate when you speak so loudly." In response to gossipers, don't contribute by adding to the gossip. Rather, add a positive comment or simply leave. In response to someone who loses their temper, step back and control your feelings until you can speak calmly. If necessary, go into another room and do something – such as breathing deeply or listening to music – to calm down.

Managers also need strategies for dealing with bad behavior because, at the workplace, it is much larger than an individual issue. In his article "Dealing with Bad Behavior at Work," Des Squire emphasizes that because of its impact on morale and profitability, managers cannot ignore it. In his article "Dealing with Acidic Attitudes: Help for Your Managers," Tom Gould identifies

these three steps for properly dealing with inappropriate behavior:
1. Be specific about what you want ("It hurts the group when you gossip. Make comments directly to the person or don't say anything.")
2. Let recipients of criticism blow off steam – they'll feel like they're being heard.
3. Avoid using "you"; use "we" instead. For example, don't say, "You have a bad attitude." Say, "We need to talk about your attitude." This reinforces that the issue is a problem for the group.

To support managers and to make employees aware of company policy, companies should have a clear "code of conduct" that defines acceptable and unacceptable behaviors. In addition, the procedures for dealing with improper behavior should be clearly spelled out in the company handbook. For example, in the case of sexual harassment, the handbook should include a definition, a process for filing a complaint, a procedure for addressing the complaint, and contact information for filing a complaint with an external organization. The company should provide each employee with a handbook at the time of hiring and provide ongoing training on company policy and procedures.

Like an infection, bad behavior spreads. Just as there is medicine for controlling infections, there are strategies for addressing bad behavior – some appropriate for individuals, some for management, and some for companies. Without strategies, there can be a negative impact on overall morale, profitability, sick leave and staff turnover.

1 Check your understanding

1. Use the reading tip to identify the main idea. Restate the main idea in your own words.
2. According to the article, how should you respond to someone speaking in a loud voice?
3. Why is it important for managers to deal with bad behavior quickly and effectively as stated in the article?
4. What does *code of conduct* mean in this article and why is it important? Write a sentence in your own words to answer this question.
5. In the second paragraph, what word means *use*?
6. In the second sentence of the third paragraph, what does *its* refer to?

2 Build your vocabulary

A Figurative language uses words or expressions with a meaning that is different from the literal meaning. The words in Column 1 below are usually used to talk about health, but in the article they refer to something else. Find the words related to health in the paragraphs indicated. Underline them. Then, in Column 2, write the phrase or sentence in the article with the health word. In Column 3, write how the literal and figurative meanings of the health words are the same.

Health word	Phrase or sentence	How are the literal and figurative meanings the same?
viruses, ¶1	*Bad behaviors and attitudes are like viruses...*	*You can catch both from someone else.*
spread, ¶1 / 5		
carrier, ¶1		
health, ¶1		
infection, ¶5		
medicine, ¶5		

B Find each of the following academic words in the article and underline the sentence.

> appropriate   ignore   reinforces   ongoing   overall   procedures

Then, on another piece of paper, copy and complete the chart.

Academic word	Phrase or sentence from article	Part of speech	Dictionary definition	My sentence
appropriate	*...some appropriate for individuals...*	*adjective*	*correct or right for a particular situation*	*Bob doesn't have appropriate clothes for his new job.*

3 Talk with a partner

Answer each question with evidence from the reading. Use one of the phrases in the Useful Language box.

> **USEFUL LANGUAGE**
> Phrases to cite examples:
> Some examples from the article are . . .
> A few examples the author included are . . .

1. What should be included in the company handbook, as stated in the article?
2. What should you do if someone loses their temper?
3. What are three things a manager can do to deal with bad attitudes at work?

> **Objective: CCR Anchor 9:** Analyze how two or more texts address similar themes or topics in order to build knowledge or to compare the approaches the authors take.

4 Analyze the texts

Review the following texts to answer the questions below: (1) Student Book, p. 66, *Bad Behavior in the Workplace*; (2) Student Book, p. 68, *Don't Let Annoying People Drive You Nuts*; (3) Extended reading, *Strategies for Dealing with Bad Behavior*.

1. Both *Bad Behavior in the Workplace* and *Strategies for Dealing with Bad Behavior* identify bad behaviors. Which two bad behaviors are addressed in both texts?
2. The authors of *Don't Let Annoying People Drive You Nuts* and *Strategies for Dealing with Bad Behavior* provide some strategies for dealing with annoying work behaviors. Identify one strategy that both authors endorse.
3. In the Randstad USA survey, what was #1 on the list of annoying workplace behaviors? What specific suggestion for this behavior was offered in *Strategies for Dealing with Bad Behavior*? What general suggestion for dealing with annoying people was offered in *Don't Let Annoying People Drive You Nuts*?
4. Two of the three texts identify a strategy that companies and other organizations can implement to help prevent bad behaviors in the workplace. Which texts are they? What are the suggested approaches in these two texts?

5 Before you write

Complete the graphic organizer with three annoying behaviors and the suggested strategies provided in the three texts. Use the information from Exercises 1–4 and evidence from the three texts.

Annoying behavior	Strategies for addressing annoying behaviors		
	Individual	**Management**	**Company/Organization**
1.			
2.			
3.			

6 Write

There is widespread agreement that annoying behaviors in the workplace can create an unhealthy environment that affects both worker satisfaction and productivity. Identify three annoying behaviors and the strategies suggested in the three texts for dealing with them. Then say whether you think the suggested strategies are effective solutions for these behaviors. Use your graphic organizer and evidence from the three texts to support your opinion.

7 After you write

A Check your writing. Did you include all the ideas in your graphic organizer?

B Share your writing with a partner.

   a. Take turns. Read your writing to your partner.

   b. Read your partner's writing to yourself. Compare it to your partner's graphic organizer.

   c. Comment on your partner's writing: Ask one question; share one thing you learned.

After reading the middle paragraphs (paragraphs 2, 3, and 4 in this article), stop and look up. Restate in your own words both the problem(s) and solution(s).

Problems with Performance Reviews

The workplace offers many challenges to both employers and employees, particularly when it comes to improving quality and efficiency. Performance reviews, also called performance appraisals or performance evaluations, were originally designed to meet this need. However, they have recently garnered criticism from both employees and supervisors.

One problem with performance reviews is that they often address too many issues, which can overwhelm the employee. In her article "4 Problems with Performance Appraisals: Where Do Managers Go Wrong?," Susan Heathfield points out that once employees hear negative feedback, they may "not hear" positive feedback. To ensure that both positive and negative feedback is heard, the appraiser can use the "sandwich" approach. In this three-step approach, appraisers (1) provide one positive comment, (2) focus on one area of concern, and (3) provide another positive point. For example, for an employee that spends too much time chatting with co-workers, the supervisor might first comment on positive feedback from customers. After that, she can comment on talking too much with co-workers and how the employee is missing deadlines. Finally, she can praise the employee for getting along well with everyone.

Another issue with performance evaluations is their subjectivity. Questions may focus on traits such as initiative or creativity, which different reviewers may evaluate differently. To avoid subjectivity, in their book *Performance Appraisals in Public Libraries,* Anne Goulding and Karen Harrison advocate "management by objectives" by focusing on behaviors, not traits (what employers want employees to do,

not what they want them to be). For example, "customer service skills" might be replaced with "level of sales," which can be measured. Reviewers should support these statements with concrete data. For example, "Your sales this quarter were ten percent less than last quarter." Reviewers not only need to be specific about the problem, but also assist workers in identifying concrete ways to improve.

Yet another difficulty with performance reviews is that they can encourage evaluators to delay feedback until the scheduled review, creating unnecessary stress on both the evaluator and the employee. For example, Jack completes a project late. If Felicia waits until his performance review to address the issue, he is unaware of her displeasure. Employees like Jack become stressed because they have had minimal feedback – positive or constructive criticism – before the review. They may shut down or react negatively, such as by becoming defensive or blaming others. Supervisors like Felicia are then upset because they feel they aren't being heard. According to Jennifer Skinner and Ravonne Green in their online article "Making the Grade: The Elements of an Effective Performance Appraisal," nothing in a performance review should be new to the person being evaluated. If Felicia had given Jack feedback when the problem occurred, it would have facilitated open communication and created a greater likelihood of improvement.

Performance reviews can be problematic for many reasons, including addressing too many issues rather than focusing on key issue(s), being subjective rather than objective, and creating undue stress because of delayed feedback.

1 Check your understanding

1. Use the reading tip to identify problems and solutions with using performance reviews. What is the author's point of view about performance reviews?
2. According to the article, how can managers avoid subjectivity?
3. According to the article, what are the three reasons employees and employers feel stress during performance reviews?
4. In your own words, explain how Felicia could have handled the evaluation process more effectively.
5. Some form of the verb *address* is in the article three times. What does *address* mean in the context of this article?
6. In the first paragraph, second sentence, what does *this need* refer to?

2 Build your vocabulary

A Often an author will use a variety of words that mean the same thing. In the paragraph indicated, find the words that have a meaning similar to the word in Column 1. Underline them in the article and write them in the chart.

Word in article	Similar words in article		
appraisers	¶3 *reviewers*	¶4 *evaluators*	
employees	¶3		
employers	¶2	¶1 / 4	
issue	¶2	¶4	¶2/3/4
performance reviews	¶1	¶1	
stressed	¶4		

B Find each of the following academic words in the article and underline the sentence.

> assist   data   evaluations   ensure   facilitated   focus

Then, on another piece of paper, copy and complete the chart.

Academic word	Phrase or sentence from article	Part of speech	Dictionary definition	My sentence
assist	*...but also assist workers in identifying concrete ways ...*	*verb*	*to help or support someone or something*	*I asked my coworker if I could assist her with the task.*

3 Talk with a partner

Answer each question with evidence from the reading.
Use one of the phrases in the Useful Language box.

1. According to the article, what is the main problem with waiting until the performance review to give feedback to an employee?
2. What is a solution the article gives to avoid the problem of waiting until the performance review to give feedback?
3. What is the main problem with employers focusing on employees traits, rather than desired accomplishments?

> **USEFUL LANGUAGE**
> Phrases to identify problems and solutions:
> The problem is . . .
> The best solution is . . .

Ventures
STUDENT'S BOOK   TRANSITIONS

> **Objective: CCR Anchor 9:** Analyze how two or more texts address similar themes or topics in order to build knowledge or to compare the approaches the authors take.

4 Analyze the texts

Review the following texts to answer the questions below: (1) Student Book, p. 76, *Accepting Criticism Gracefully*; (2) Student Book, p. 78, *The Performance Evaluation*; (3) Extended reading, *Problems with Performance Reviews*.

1. Both *Accepting Criticism Gracefully* and *The Performance Evaluation* describe what happens to employees when they hear unexpected negative criticism. Describe the feelings that are discussed in the articles.

2. The *Performance Evaluation* describes John's experience with his negative performance evaluation. *Accepting Criticism Gracefully* provides specific steps that would help John deal with this situation. Briefly describe the four steps.

3. In *The Performance Evaluation*, John said, "If I had known he was so displeased with my work, I would have been more prepared for the criticism." Paragraph 4 of *Problems with Performance Reviews* reinforces why this may have been difficult for Jack. Restate the problem and solution.

4. What new problem and solution were presented in *Problems with Performance Reviews* that was not raised in the other two texts?

5 Before you write

Complete the graphic organizer with three problems with performance reviews. Say how it is a problem for employees and employers. Then give the solutions suggested for each problem for both employers and employees. Use the information from Exercises 1–4 and evidence from the three texts to complete the graphic organizer.

Problem 1 _____ **Employees** _____ **Employer** _____	**Solution 1** _____ **Employees** _____ **Employer** _____
Problem 2 _____ **Employees** _____ **Employer** _____	**Solution 2** _____ **Employees** _____ **Employer** _____
Problem 3 _____ **Employees** _____ **Employer** _____	**Solution 3** _____ **Employees** _____ **Employer** _____

6 Write

Performance reviews are common, but there are a number of problems with them for both employers and employees. Discuss three problems with performance reviews and give solutions to the problems. Use your graphic organizer and evidence from the three texts to write a problem / solution essay.

7 After you write

A Check your writing. Did you include all the ideas in your graphic organizer?

B Share your writing with a partner.

    a. Take turns. Read your writing to your partner.

    b. Read your partner's writing to yourself. Compare it to your partner's graphic organizer.

    c. Comment on your partner's writing: Ask one question; share one thing you learned.

Before you read the entire article, read the first paragraph. Then identify the author's purpose.

The Problem with Optimism

One definition of optimism is "expecting the most favorable of outcomes or conditions." In contrast, pessimists anticipate the worst. Since the publication of *The Power of Positive Thinking* (Peale, 1996), thinking positively has become a mantra and thinking negatively has been considered a major reason for failure. But are the outcomes from optimism always good? Let's consider the downsides of looking on the bright side.

One drawback to too much optimism is the potential that not facing reality can create negative consequences. Let's take health as an example. Someone who assumes that optimism can cure a toothache, a headache, or even a serious illness such as cancer, may not take action beyond positive thinking. This delay can allow symptoms to worsen rather than improve. Susan Webber, founder of a management-consulting firm, says people must acknowledge potential problems if they are going to make realistic, objective assessments. The trick is finding a balance between optimism and reality.

Another problem with optimism is lack of critical thinking. According to researchers at the University of New South Wales, negative thinkers are more successful than optimists at using the critical part of their brain. Their research indicates that negative thinkers "think more clearly, make fewer mistakes . . . and are better at decision making." Based on this research, James Adonis, author of "The Benefits of Negative Thinking" in *The Sydney Morning Herald*, recommends that those who work with negative thinkers should seek their opinion because they have probably picked up on things that others have missed. He indicates that their ideas and solutions can be valuable, so others who are making decisions should consult them. The research also showed benefits to positive thinking, but the researchers concluded that negative thinking shouldn't be ignored; there's a place for both in the workplace.

Yet another consequence of perpetual optimism is its potential for negatively impacting others. For instance, when positivity results in failing to address problems, it can ultimately demotivate others. For example, at work, rather than addressing bad work habits – such as lack of punctuality and inattention to detail – with employees, a supervisor covers with undeserved praise. Conscientious employees may lose their motivation to do good work. At school, a teacher might also "sweep bad behavior under the rug," which is unfair and discouraging to the students who are diligent and hardworking.

Let's return to the question asked at the beginning: Are the outcomes from optimism always good? Clearly, too much optimism can have negative consequences, sometimes for the optimist and sometimes for the person receiving feedback from the optimist. Furthermore, optimists, inclined to expect the best, don't always think critically the way pessimists do. As a result, the world needs both optimists and pessimists.

1 Check your understanding

1. After you read the first paragraph, explain the author's purpose in your own words.
2. According to the article, how can too much optimism result in negative consequences for someone who is sick?
3. According to the article, why does the author of "The Benefits of Negative Thinking" suggest having negative thinkers as part of a work team?
4. Give an example from the article of how perpetual optimism can demotivate others.
5. In the second paragraph, what word means *problem*?
6. In the second sentence of the fourth paragraph, what does *it* refer to?

2 Build your vocabulary

A Antonyms are words that mean the opposite of each other. Find the antonyms of the words in Column 1 in the paragraph indicated. Then complete the chart.

Word	Antonym (from the article)	Phrase where the word occurs
1. criticize	¶4 *praise*	*...with employees, a supervisor covers with undeserved praise.*
2. deserved	¶4	
3. improve	¶2	
4. motivate	¶4	
5. subjective	¶2	
6. passing	¶4	
7. tardiness	¶4	
8. unfavorable	¶1	

B Find each of the following academic words in the article and underline the sentence.

> acknowledge   assessments   assumes   consequence(s)   inclined   ultimately

Then, on another piece of paper, copy and complete the chart.

Academic word	Phrase or sentence from article	Part of speech	Dictionary definition	My sentence
acknowledge	*...people must acknowledge potential problems*	*verb*	*to recognize as true*	*The student acknowledged that she made a mistake.*

3 Talk with a partner

Answer each question with evidence from the reading.
Use one of the phrases in the Useful Language box.

1. Is being very optimistic during an illness always a good thing?
2. Are negative thinkers different from optimistic thinkers?
3. Does continuous optimism have a negative impact on others?

> **USEFUL LANGUAGE**
> Phrases to provide evidence for an opinion:
> I believe that _____ because . . .
> I think that _____ because . . .

Ventures
2ⁿᵈ Edition
STUDENT'S BOOK
TRANSITIONS

> **Objective: CCR Anchor 9:** Analyze how two or more texts address similar themes or topics in order to build knowledge or to compare the approaches the authors take.

4 Analyze the texts

Review the following texts to answer the questions below: (1) Student Book, p. 86, *The Power of Positive Thinking*; (2) Student Book, p. 88, *Say No to Negativitis*; (3) Extended reading, *The Problem with Optimism*.

1. The author of *The Power of Positive Thinking* describes how Hugo Abitbol survived cancer and now volunteers to raise cancer awareness. He is quoted as saying ". . . if you have the right attitude, positive things will happen." Considering the drawback of optimism discussed in paragraph 2 of *The Problem with Optimism*, what are the dangers in Hugo's attitude?

2. The article *Say No to Negativitis* provides some suggestions for avoiding negativity in the workplace. What step seems to support what Hugo did in his own life to keep moving forward?

3. How is negativity described differently in *Say No to Negativitis* and in what researchers discuss in *The Problem with Optimism?*

4. What new consequence of constant optimism was presented in *The Problem with Optimism* that was not offered in the other two texts? Restate the workplace example of this consequence in your own words.

5 Before you write

Do you agree or disagree that there are both benefits and drawbacks to positive thinking? Take a stand and convince others of your position. Use the information from Exercises 1–4 and evidence from the three texts to complete the graphic organizer.

Main Reason 1	Main Reason 2	Main Reason 3

Evidence / Example	Evidence / Example	Evidence / Example

6 Write

Do you agree or disagree that there are both benefits and drawbacks to positive thinking? Take a stand and convince others of your position. Use your graphic organizer and evidence from the three texts to write a persuasive paragraph / essay.

7 After you write

A Check your writing. Did you include all the ideas in your graphic organizer?

B Share your writing with a partner.

   a. Take turns. Read your writing to your partner.

   b. Read your partner's writing to yourself. Compare it to your partner's graphic organizer.

   c. Comment on your partner's writing: Ask one question; share one thing you learned.

Before you read the entire article, read the first and last paragraphs to identify the author's point of view.

The Limits of Email

Email is an effective tool for people who need to exchange ideas and information remotely or across time zones. A study by Arvey ("Why Face-to-Face Business Meetings Matter") documents that email is one of the most prevalent forms of communication used by Hilton Hotel businesspeople in various countries. Although there are many benefits to email, it should not become our core means of communication.

One negative impact caused by email is how it has discouraged regular human contact. According to Straus and McGrath (*Does the medium matter? The interaction of task type and technology on group performance and member reactions. http://www.ncbi.nlm.nih. gov/pubmed/8200874*), group processes and outcomes that require coordination, consensus, timing, and/or persuasion of others are more effectively accomplished in a face-to-face meeting than they are over email. For instance, if a team of students has to design a complex project that has several aspects, the students may find it much more efficient to initially meet and detail the goals of the project and coordinate who will do what. This kind of face-to-face meeting may help some team members feel more engaged in the project and promote consensus among members about the goals and timelines.

If an issue arises that needs to be addressed confidentially, emails are a particularly bad mode of communication. An email chain between someone and their former, disgruntled boss, which perhaps escalated to threats and other inappropriate language, could be used as evidence in a civil suit. Company secrets could be forwarded to a competitor either intentionally or unintentionally. A student could send another student what he thinks is a confidential email about the lack of participation by a team member only to discover it has been forwarded to the person the email is about. Anything confidential is best reserved for in-person communication to protect all parties involved.

The majority of digital communication platforms, including email, lack expression, sensory stimulation, and tone of voice, which indicates attitude, feeling, and emotion. Without such cues, messages can seem especially harsh, such as in an email from a supervisor warning an otherwise great employee about a missed deadline or work that needs to be revised. With misinterpretation, there is also the potential for serious consequences. For instance, a joke sent by email, if interpreted as serious, might result in animosity between co-workers or friends.

Emails are undeniably effective tools of communication. The demands of global businesses and physically detached workplaces make email integral to business today. However, a reliance on email as the primary mode of communication is a dangerous trend: it is not effective in situations that require group processes, its confidentiality can be compromised, and it has potential for misinterpretation.

UNIT 10

1 Check your understanding

1. Use the reading tip to identify the author's point of view. Restate the author's point of view in your own words.
2. According to the article, why shouldn't confidential matters be discussed over email?
3. According to the author, what happens more effectively in face-to-face meetings than through email communication?
4. According to paragraph four, what can cause people to misinterpret email messages?
5. Both the first and last paragraphs have words that mean "not close, distant" or "separate, not attached." What are the two words?
6. In the fourth paragraph, what phrase signals that an example is following?

2 Build your vocabulary

A The following words have multiple meanings. Find the words in Column 1 in the paragraph indicated and underline them. Then circle the definition that is used in the context of the article.

Word	1st meaning	2nd meaning	3rd meaning
1. tool, ¶1	a handheld device that aids in accomplishing a task	anything that helps you to do what you want to do	an element of a computer program that activates and controls a particular function
2. chain, ¶3	a length of metal rings that are connected together	a group of stores	a set of connected or related things
3. core, ¶1	the hard, central part of some fruits	the central or most important part of something	the center of the Earth
4. exchange, ¶1	to give or receive something in place of another	a money transfer between two currencies	a store or shop specializing in merchandise usually of a particular type
5. issue, ¶2	an unsettled matter, usually a concern or problem	a particular copy of a magazine or newspaper	to give, supply, or produce something
6. suit, ¶2	the four groups of playing cards in a pack that have the same symbol	a legal action in a court of law to settle a disagreement	a set of clothes, such as a jacket, pants, or skirt, that match

B Find each of the following academic words in the article and underline the sentence.

> coordinate   design   evidence   integral   misinterpretation   promote

Then, on another piece of paper, copy and complete the chart.

Academic word	Phrase or sentence from article	Part of speech	Dictionary definition	My sentence
coordinate	. . . coordinate who will do what.	verb	to work or act together properly and well	Nurses and doctors must coordinate if surgery is going to be successful.

3 Talk with a partner

Cite evidence from the text to answer the questions. Use one of the phrases in the Useful Language box.

1. What does Arvey say about email?
2. In your own words, report what Straus and McGrath's views are concerning email.
3. How has email discouraged human contact?

USEFUL LANGUAGE
Phrases to identify a source:
[Title of source] reports that . . .
[Author's name] reports that . . .

4 Analyze the texts

Review the following texts to answer the questions below: (1) Student Book, p. 96, *Email Etiquette 101*; (2) Student Book, p. 98, *Good Business Writing Doesn't Beat Around the Bush*; (3) Extended Reading, *The Limits of Email*.

1. The authors of *Email Etiquette 101* and *The Limits of Email* report an increased use of email. Identify data from both texts that document this increase.
2. Authors of *Email Etiquette 101* and *The Limits of Email* both warn about the same problem with email messages. Identify the problem described in the texts.
3. The authors of *Email Etiquette 101* and *The Limits of Email* also discuss issues with forwarding emails. Identify the issues each describes.
4. The author of *Good Business Writing Doesn't Beat Around the Bush* describes the K.I.S.S. technique for business communication. Restate the K.I.S.S. technique in your own words. Would using the K.I.S.S. technique solve the issues described in paragraph two of *The Limits of Email*? Use evidence from the texts to support your answer.

5 Before you write

Because email communication is prevalent in business and among Internet users, it is especially important to use it appropriately and strategically. Do you agree or disagree? Take a stand and convince others of your position. Use the information from Exercises 1–4 and evidence from the three texts to complete the graphic organizer.

Main Reason 1	Main Reason 2	Main Reason 3

Evidence / Example	Evidence / Example	Evidence / Example

6 Write

Because email communication is prevalent in business and among Internet users, it is especially important to use it appropriately and strategically. Do you agree or disagree? Take a stand and convince others of your position. Use your graphic organizer and evidence from the three texts to support your opinion.

7 After you write

A Check your writing. Did you include all the ideas in your graphic organizer?

B Share your writing with a partner.
   a. Take turns. Read your writing to your partner.
   b. Read your partner's writing to yourself. Compare it to your partner's graphic organizer.
   c. Comment on your partner's writing: Ask one question; share one thing you learned.

AUDIO SCRIPT

Unit 1 Lesson A

Page 3, Exercises 2A and 2B – CD1 Track 2

Good afternoon, everyone.
I understand that some of you will start looking for a job as soon as this course finishes, and others plan to get some more training first . . . maybe go to college or sign up for vocational classes . . .
So, today I want to talk about a topic that's very important for all of you, and that is the kinds of skills and qualities that you will need to get a job in today's competitive economy . . . Basically, there are two types of skills you will need if you want to be successful. The first type is called "hard skills," and the second type is called "soft skills."
"Hard skills" are the technical skills and the knowledge you need in order to do a job. These are things you can learn in school or on the job. For example, if you want to be a pharmacy technician, you will need to learn the names of medications, how to use a cash register, how to take messages from doctors, and so on. If your goal is to get a job in a factory, then you need to learn how to use the machines and maybe how to operate a computer. These are hard skills.
"Soft skills" are a little harder to define. They include your personal qualities and what we call your "people skills." For example, are you hardworking, motivated, reliable, and enthusiastic?
Do you communicate well with your classmates and co-workers? Do customers like you and trust you? Those are examples of soft skills.
Sometimes people ask me what's more important, hard skills or soft skills. Well, both of them are important, but I think soft skills are probably more important, because they're harder to teach and because they are transferable . . . I mean, you can take them with you from job to job. If you have a good attitude and you communicate well, you will be successful in any job you have.

Page 6, Exercise 2 – CD1 Track 3

Setting Goals for the Future
What do you want your future to look like? Do you want to develop skills for a better job? Do you want to graduate from college? No matter what you want in the future, one of the best ways to get there is by setting goals.

Setting a goal means making a decision about what you want to achieve. It requires finding out what you need to do to achieve that goal and planning how long it will take you to do it.
Making choices about the future can be difficult because we often focus only on the present. In order to think about your future goals, take a few minutes and imagine what you want your life to be like in one, two, or three years. Where will you be? What will you be doing? How will you feel?
There are a number of important points for you to keep in mind when setting a goal. It should be detailed, measurable, and realistic, and it should have a completion date.
Once you have a goal in mind, try to add as much detail as possible. Adding detail will make the goal clearer. For example, instead of saying "I want to get a better job," you can add details, such as "I want to study cooking so that I can be a chef." Details like "study cooking" and "be a chef" clearly show what you want to achieve and how you plan to achieve it.
In addition to adding detail to your goal, make sure you can measure your progress. "I want a better education" is a good goal, but it is difficult to measure. How will you know when your goal is completed? "I will apply to three colleges next spring" is a better goal because you can pay attention to your progress.
Goals should be challenging, but they should not be too difficult. An impossible goal will lead to failure. You can avoid failure by making sure your goal is realistic. Becoming a professional soccer player might be your dream, but is it realistic? Instead, set your goal on something more achievable, like playing for a local team.
Finally, make sure your goal has a completion date, or deadline. If you know when you want to complete your goal, you will be more motivated. Without a deadline, people often stop paying attention to their goal. Just as your goal should be realistic, your deadline should be realistic also.

Page 8, Exercise 2 – CD1 Track 4

Keys for Success at Work
Many people think that employers are only interested in technical skills when they interview new candidates for a job; however, in today's job market, most companies are looking for much more. Different companies have different needs,

yet there are a number of general skills and qualities they all hope to find. These skills include:

Communication skills – Companies are interested in people who can communicate and get along well with others. The way you organize your thoughts, express your ideas, and deal positively with customers and co-workers is what will impress employers the most.

Leadership skills – Many companies ask for people who are "self-starters" and who are willing to lead others. In other words, employers want people who can think for themselves and who aren't afraid to make independent decisions.

Maturity – A mature employee is someone who manages time well, takes responsibility for mistakes, and does not become frustrated in challenging situations.

Problem-solving skills – Problem-solving and critical-thinking skills are also very important to employers. Companies value employees who are able to recognize problems, develop a plan for solving them, and follow through with that plan.

Commitment – Employers prefer workers who work hard toward the company's goals. They want to hire team players who are committed to their jobs.

Informational skills – Your ability to gather, organize, and analyze information is very important in today's world. Knowing how to use a computer to search the Internet, send emails, and solve problems is key in almost every profession.
As you can see, most of these do not involve technical skills. They are "people skills" that are important in every job or field. If you lack any of these skills or qualities, you should look for ways to develop them as part of your goal setting for the future.

Unit 2 Lesson A

Page 13, Exercises 2A and 2B – CD1 Track 5

I'd like to describe two different workers for you, David and Sarah, and while I'm talking about them I'd like you to think about which one got a promotion. OK?
So, David and Sarah, they work together in a busy office. Both of them are dedicated to their jobs; they're conscientious and loyal, but their personalities are very different. David is a motivated, optimistic person who enjoys taking on new

challenges. It's true that sometimes he works too quickly and makes mistakes, but when this happens, he thinks of it as a learning experience and promises himself that he'll do better next time. All right, now Sarah, on the other hand, judges herself very negatively if she makes a mistake.

Although she's really smart and works hard, she often worries that she is not doing a good job, and her feelings are easily hurt when anyone criticizes her. Sarah's expectations of herself are unrealistically high, so she's easily disappointed.

OK, so, which worker do you think got the promotion? David, obviously. He's happy and enthusiastic about his new responsibilities, while Sarah, yeah, as you can probably guess, feels like a failure.

Page 16, Exercise 2 – CD1 Track 6

Understanding Self-Confidence
What Is Self-Confidence?
Self-confidence means believing in yourself and your abilities. It means being ready and willing to face new situations and accomplish difficult tasks. Self-confident people are usually eager, assertive, motivated, willing to accept criticism, emotionally mature, optimistic, and productive. People who don't have self-confidence lack the inner belief in their ability to be successful. They tend to be withdrawn, unmotivated, overly sensitive to criticism, distrustful, and pessimistic. They don't feel good about themselves. Often they feel like failures.
What Affects Self-Confidence?
Self-confidence is affected by life experiences. You are influenced by parents, siblings, friends, and teachers. From them, you learn how to think about yourself and the world around you. It is the support and encouragement you receive from the people around you – or the lack of it – that helps shape your inner feelings about yourself. A nurturing environment that provides positive feedback improves self-confidence. People learn by making mistakes, and they need to feel that missteps along the way are to be expected. However, when friends, family, and others offer unfair criticism, hold unrealistic expectations, or put too much pressure on a person, self-confidence can be affected.
Several different types of behavior show a lack of self-confidence:

1. You judge yourself or your abilities too harshly, or you are overly critical of your performance.
2. You focus too much on your failures and see them as negative events instead of learning experiences.
3. You place too much pressure or stress on yourself to succeed.
4. You set goals that are unrealistic and above your abilities.
5. You are fearful of not succeeding or making mistakes.

A lack of self-confidence can often keep people from achieving their full potential. That's why it's important to get help if you are affected by this problem.

Page 18, Exercise 2 – CD1 Track 7

Building Self-Confidence
How Do You Build Self-Confidence?
Self-confidence is not built overnight. It is a process that begins by first understanding why you lack confidence, then taking active steps to change your negative thinking and behaviors into positive ones.
First, think about why you lack confidence. Perhaps you are unhappy with your appearance, your social or academic achievements, or the way a relationship ended. Try to identify these feelings and perhaps talk about them with someone you trust. It may surprise you that others share the same kinds of self-doubts or have ones of their own. See your fears as challenges you can overcome – don't let them have power over you!

Steps to Building Self-Confidence
Think of building self-confidence as a process. Aim to make small, positive steps toward success. Practice these strategies until they become your new habits.

1. Think about your good qualities. Are you conscientious, loyal, reliable, and cooperative? Recognize your talents and abilities; these will help you feel better about yourself.
2. Think positively about yourself and what you set out to do. Negative thoughts lead to worry, which can confuse you and keep you from achieving success.
3. Set realistic goals that you can truly reach, both large and small. Praise yourself when you reach even the smallest goals, but keep striving for the bigger ones.
4. Focus on your successes and not on your failures. Realize that everyone makes mistakes, and let yours be tools for learning.
5. Be assertive. It is essential for people to express their thoughts, feelings, and emotions to others. You are entitled to your opinion, and you have important things to say. Don't be afraid to say them.
6. Find a creative outlet for self-expression. Find an activity that lets your abilities shine, such as music, art, cooking, crafts, or sports. You don't have to be the best at what you do, but the risks you take and the things you create provide a fast route to greater self-acceptance.

Unit 3

Page 23, Exercises 2A and 2B – CD1 Track 8

The topic of our class today is volunteering, or working to help others without getting paid for it. According to the U.S. government, about 26 percent of Americans volunteer at least once a year, and I'm sure you know people who volunteer much more often, maybe even once a week.

If you've ever volunteered anywhere, then you know that volunteering can be a very beneficial experience. Although you don't earn money, you can learn a lot about the world of work. Volunteering can be a type of on-the-job training. Also, you can meet wonderful people and feel good about helping them.

There are all kinds of places to volunteer, and each place is looking for people with different abilities. If you are interested in working with children, you could become a tutor and help them with their homework, or volunteer in a day-care center. If you enjoy working with elderly people, you could volunteer your time in a nursing home. If you like building things, you could volunteer for an organization that builds low-cost housing for people who don't have much money. Other volunteer work you might be interested in could be, removing graffiti from public places, or working at a food bank to put together food boxes or baskets for low-income families.

Volunteer work can also take you overseas. If you're interested in working in other countries, you could become a language tutor or, if you have medical skills, you could volunteer to help in health clinics around the world, like so many doctors did following the earthquake in Haiti in 2010.

So whether you're volunteering to gain experience for a job or you just want to help others, there are many opportunities for you to be involved in your local community or the larger global community.

Page 26, Exercise 2 – CD1 Track 9

Volunteering the Family Way
For sisters Sarah and Audrey Granger of central Missouri, school and volunteering go hand in hand. Community college sophomore Sarah was recently made

Student Coordinator for Recycling at her school – a new, paid position for the college. She immediately started to work by developing a central recycling site, ordering new collection bins for campus buildings, and recruiting her younger sister, Audrey, to be her first volunteer.

Audrey, in her first year at the college, wasn't sure she had time for a volunteer job. With all her classes, she said, she thought it would be too much work. "But after working with Sarah and learning how to collect and organize the material for recycling, I discovered it was easier than I thought," she said.

Because of the instant popularity of the recycling project, Audrey said that she quickly understood the value of her volunteer work. "I started to get the idea that you could make a difference and, after a while, reusing and recycling just became part of my lifestyle."

As coordinator of the campus-wide program, Sarah supervises four volunteers, including her sister. The team has worked hard to introduce recycled paper products in the cafeteria and to use plant waste as compost material in the college's gardens. "It's better to reuse some of the food waste from the cafeteria instead of dumping it in the community landfill," Audrey explained.

For Sarah, who is majoring in environmental studies, the position of Student Coordinator is a perfect way to combine her passion for the environment and her interest in volunteering. She said she became interested in volunteering as a child. "My mother works for Habitat for Humanity," she said, "and I used to spend a lot of time helping her with her projects."

In order to keep the recycling program "going and growing," Sarah said people need to use it and support it as much as possible. With committed volunteers like her sister Audrey, there's no doubt that the program has a bright future.

Page 28, Exercise 2 – CD1 Track 10

Volunteering While at College

It's no secret that college students have busy lives. Classes, jobs, and studying often leave very little free time for anything else.

Despite their schedules, however, college students are volunteering more than ever, according to a 2006 study by the Corporation for National and Community Services. In fact, the study said college students are more likely to participate in volunteer activities than other people their age not enrolled in college.

There are many benefits to volunteering while in college. First of all, in many states students can get college credit for helping local organizations. In Massachusetts, for example, many students at Holyoke Community College volunteer at community organizations. In return for their good deeds, the students receive credit and are one step closer to graduating.

In order to volunteer for credit, students need to first talk to their advisor. They often need to provide information about the work and the number of hours it will take. The volunteer work is typically related to the student's major.

A second benefit is that volunteering can help satisfy college requirements. At the University of California, Santa Barbara, honor students must volunteer for at least 20 hours during their last two years on campus. This "community-service requirement" is becoming more and more common in schools across the country.

A third benefit to volunteering involves getting a job. Volunteer work looks great on a graduate's résumé. When an employer sees community service on your résumé, it says you want to help others and are curious about the world around you. These characteristics can help get you an interview.

Whether you volunteer for credit, to meet a requirement, or to improve your résumé, keep in mind the most important aspect of community service: making a difference.

Unit 4

Page 33, Exercises 2A and 2B – CD1 Track 11

I know that some of you haven't ever had a job before, especially if you're a full-time student, so I thought I'd start our workshop today by giving you an overview of the main steps in the job search process. It can be a long process, so let me encourage you to stop by the campus career center anytime if you need help, OK?

OK. So the first step in finding a job is deciding what type of job you'd like to have. What are your interests? What are your hobbies? What are you good at? What kind of experience do you have? It's good to write these things down, and then ask yourself, "What kind of job fits my interests and abilities?"

Next, start looking for jobs in your area. One of the best ways to find out about job openings is by word of mouth – you know, through talking to friends, neighbors, and family members. Look online, and check out the listings at the campus career center. You can also look in the newspaper, of course.

The third step is filling out applications for the jobs you're interested in. For most jobs these days, you can find applications online, or else you can go to the workplace itself. Fill out the job application carefully and don't lie!

Fourth, if you're asked to give references, ask your previous employers to give you a recommendation. If you've never worked before, think of a trusted friend or teacher who knows you well and would be a good personal reference for you.

Next, you'll also need to write a resume to send with your application. We'll talk about resume writing at our next meeting.

Finally, depending on the type of job you are applying for, you may need to write a cover letter to send in with your job application and resume. A personalized letter that tells an employer how much you are interested in the job could make all the difference in getting an invitation to come for an interview.

And speaking of interviews . . . the hardest thing, after you've done all the things we've just talked about, is waiting for the phone call asking you to come in for an interview. While you're waiting, make good use of your time. Keep studying and developing your skills. If you do these things, I promise that sooner or later you'll find a good job.

Page 36, Exercise 2 – CD1 Track 12

Online Job Searches: Beware of Scammers!

CONSIDER THESE EXPERIENCES of people applying for jobs on the Internet:

- John applies for a teaching job he found online. He sends in his résumé and some personal information that the employer had requested. Later, John gets a call from his bank saying someone had used the Internet to steal money from his bank account.
- Sophia answers an ad for a salesperson that she saw on a job-search Web site. She later learns that the information she had given allowed someone to illegally use her credit card number.

These are just two examples of a new way of stealing: using false Internet job listings to gain people's personal information. As more employers see the Internet as an easy and inexpensive way to reach larger numbers of applicants, scammers, or those who use tricks and deception to get private information from people, see an easy way to make money.

Scammers place false ads online to cheat inexperienced job applicants into revealing their personal information.

Believing they are applying for a real job, applicants sometimes give out their social security, student ID, or bank account numbers, their credit card information, or their mother's maiden name. Providing this information allows scammers to steal money from people or make illegal purchases.

The lesson to those who use the Internet to apply for jobs is this: Be cautious! Be wary of online ads that do not mention the company name or that offer a salary that seems too good to be true. These ads may be false.

Before giving any personal information, do some research to see if the company you are dealing with is real. Scammers can set up false Web sites, so phone, send an email, or visit the office before sending in your résumé. Be careful when you give your personal information to an employer online.

Using the Internet to apply for jobs is convenient, but it is up to you to make sure the job you're applying for is real and the company offering the job is honest.

Page 38, Exercise 2 – CD1 Track 13

Ten Tips for a Great Job Application

Why is knowing how to fill out a job application properly so important? For many job seekers, the job application is their letter of introduction. A neatly done, complete application will catch the eye and the interest of a potential new employer, while a messy, incomplete one is much more likely to end up in the trash. Here are ten tips for completing a job application successfully:

1. **Be prepared.** Collect important documents like your student ID, driver's license, social security number, and résumé, and put these things in a folder for easy access. Also include contact information for your previous employers, your rate of pay, and references.
2. **Follow instructions.** Take time to read the entire application before you fill it out. Figure out what information is required in each section. Completing the application correctly is the first test of your ability to follow directions.
3. **Type accurately.** The application is a reflection of you, so be sure to go over it for "typos" and careless grammar mistakes.
4. **Target the job.** Answer questions with the particular job in mind. Be specific. Include experience and education that matches the requirements of the job that you are applying for.

5. **Answer ALL questions.** Fill out the application completely; don't leave anything blank. If a question doesn't apply to your situation, write N/A or not applicable. This will show the employer you are careful.
6. **Be honest.** Be truthful in the application. Information here will become part of your employment history and, if you lie, someone is sure to find out. You could lose your job. However, do not offer more information than you are asked to give.
7. **Don't be negative.** Your goal is to get an interview, so play up your strengths and say only positive things about yourself.
8. **Salary required.** Don't type in a number for salary questions. Instead write "Open." This shows a positive attitude toward discussions about your pay.
9. **Gaps in employment.** It is OK to have gaps in your work history. Entering information like "returned to school," "moved," or "volunteered" are all acceptable reasons for gaps.
10. **Proofread.** Reread your application several times before sending it.

Following these guidelines will make it more likely that a potential employer will read your application from beginning to end. A well-done application doesn't guarantee you will get a job, but it certainly increases your chances.

Unit 5

Page 43, Exercises 2A and 2B – CD1 Track 14

When people meet for the first time, how long do you think it takes them to form their first impression of each other? Five minutes? One minute? Would you believe . . . three seconds or less?

That's right, three seconds for someone to look you over and evaluate you when they meet you for the first time. And, research shows, once someone forms an opinion of you, there's almost nothing you can do to change their minds. So because first impressions are so important, in the next few minutes I want to give you five simple rules for making a great first impression, whether at work or in a social situation. Ready?

Rule number one in North American culture is – be on time. If your job interview is set for 9:00 a.m., try to get there early, at 8:45. If someone invites

you for dinner for 7 o'clock, it's OK to arrive at 7:15, but any later than that and your host might think you are rude – and that's not the way to make a good first impression.

Rule number two, and again I'm talking about American culture, is – smile! A smile makes you seem warm and open, and research even shows smiling can improve your health and your mood. There's nothing like a smile to create a good first impression.

My third rule is – pay attention to your body language. Stand up straight, make eye contact, and greet your new acquaintance with a firm handshake. These behaviors will make you seem confident and attractive, and they will make it easy for people to remember you.

Rule number four is – learn people's names. If it's hard for you to pronounce a name, it's OK to ask the person to repeat it. And then, do your best to use the person's name during your first conversation. Doing this will give the impression that you are polite and truly interested in getting to know the other person.

And finally, focus all your attention on the person you're meeting. Have you ever been introduced to someone who, in the middle of the introduction, excused themselves to answer their cell phone? Remember, the person in front of you is always more important than the person calling you on the phone. If you want to make a good first impression, turn off your cell phone and give your new acquaintance 100 percent of your attention.

If you follow these five rules, I promise that you will make a good first impression on everyone you meet.
Good luck!

Page 46, Exercise 2 – CD1 Track 15

Keys to a Successful Interview

What makes for a successful interview? Consider the experiences of these two job interviewees:

Carlos leaves for a job interview in plenty however, he doesn't consider rush-hour traffic and ends up arriving ten minutes late. He opens his bag, sees no papers, and realizes that he left his résumé at home. Carlos is flustered, and while shaking the interviewer's hand, he mispronounces the woman's name.

Sheila takes the time to research the company she is applying to and comes to her interview well prepared. But when the interviewer asks if she had any problems at her last job, she gives a full description of how all her former co-workers were lazy and unmotivated and how she hated working there.

Neither Carlos nor Sheila got the job. Could they have done things differently to get a better outcome?

These scenarios illustrate an important fact: Interviewing skills are essential to creating the kind of positive impression you want to make on the person interviewing you. So instead of thinking about what you should have done to make your last interview go better, consider the following list of important dos and don'ts before your next interview:

DO:
✓ Prepare the materials you need ahead of time.
✓ Arrive early.
✓ Learn the name of the person who is interviewing you.
✓ Learn something about the company, school, or organization beforehand.
✓ Be honest about your skills, education, and experience.
✓ Be positive and interested.
✓ Follow up with a thank-you note.

DON'T:
✗ Wear inappropriate clothing.
✗ Ask about the salary right away.
✗ Be overly nervous.
✗ Speak negatively about others.
✗ Chew gum or smell like smoke.
✗ Act desperate for the position.

Page 48, Exercise 2 – CD1 Track 16

Make the Most of Your Interview - Follow Up!

Let's say you've just had an interview for an on-campus position or with a new company. Now what? Do you just keep checking your email, waiting by the phone, or searching the mail for a letter offering you the position (or not)? Is there anything more you can do to improve the odds of getting the position?

Unfortunately, chances are that there were dozens, if not hundreds, of other applicants for the job or position to which you just applied. And many of the applicants brought the same kinds of skills, experience, and attitude you did to the interview. So the real question is – How do you make yourself stand out from the crowd?

The answer lies in the realization that the interview is not over when you walk out of the interviewer's office. You must follow up.

Sending a thank-you note after your meeting can help you make the most of your interview. A simple note or email thanking the company for considering you

for the position or for the chance to meet some of the people involved is a great way to remind the interviewer that you are truly motivated and interested. It also shows that you have good manners.

A thank-you note is appropriate whether or not you felt the interview was successful. If it went well, a thank-you note may persuade the interviewer to select you over other competing candidates. If it did not go well, the note can help the interviewer remember you favorably even if you are not selected.

At the end of your interview, the interviewer should have told you how to follow up and whom to contact. If not, just address the thank-you note to him or her. Write the note soon after the interview to improve the chance that the interviewer will remember you.

It is important to send only one follow-up email or note. If you do not get a response, then you can assume you did not get the position. Don't send any more follow-up notes; you will become an annoyance, and that is not your goal. Instead, be prepared to move on to the next new opportunity. Don't focus on what could have been, but on what may still lie ahead.

Unit 6

Page 53, Exercises 2A and 2B – CD2 Track 2

I'd like to spend some time today talking about small talk. Now, I know this is a subject that many of you are very interested in, because the rules of conversation are quite different in your home cultures. Students are always asking me, "What is small talk? When do we do it, and why?" and "Which topics are OK to talk about?" So let me start by giving some general answers to those questions.

So, first of all, what is small talk? Well, it's a kind of casual or "light" conversation about neutral or non-controversial subjects like the weather or sports. It's the kind of conversation we have with people in places like parties, or standing in line somewhere, or when we're waiting for a class or a business meeting to start. One purpose of small talk is to "break the ice," which means to start a conversation with another person, especially a person you don't know very well. It's a polite way to start talking with someone, and often it's a bridge to talking about bigger topics later, when you feel more comfortable with each other. Another purpose of small talk is to fill the time before the start of an event like a meeting or a class.

OK, so let's say you're at a party with a bunch of people you don't know very well, and you need to make small talk. What should you talk about, and which topics should you avoid?

"Safe" topics include the weather and sports, as I said; also anything about your native country or your language, your family, traveling, or learning English. Movies, music, and entertainment are also good topics.

Now, inappropriate topics are things that Americans consider to be private, so religion, politics, sex, and money – you shouldn't ask questions about those things until you know people very well. You should never ask Americans how much money they make or what they paid for something. It's also inappropriate to make negative comments about people's bodies, like saying they've gained weight or that they look sick.

Remember, the purpose of small talk is to open up a conversation and to get to know another person. Don't start out by talking about subjects that are too personal or too heavy. If you approach another person with respect, and you are careful about the subjects you choose to speak about, people will feel comfortable around you. It's also a great way to practice your English!

Page 56, Exercise 2 – CD2 Track 3

Small Talk, Big Problems

Marco, a new immigrant from Chile, works in a factory during the day and takes college classes at night. Shortly after starting at work and at school, he has two confusing experiences:

- One evening, he sees an American student from one of his classes walking toward him. As the student comes closer, Marco says, "Hi." The student responds with "Hi, how are you?" But instead of waiting for Marco's answer, the student keeps on walking. Marco is confused and wonders, "Why does my classmate dislike me?"
- At the factory, Marco sits down to have lunch with a group of co-workers. He introduces himself and talks a bit about his family, and his co-workers do the same. At the end of lunch, an American co-worker says, "It was nice to meet you, Marco. Let's get together sometime." A week goes by. Marco sees the woman every day, but she never talks about seeing him or getting together with him outside of work. Marco wonders, "Why did she lie to me?"

Are Marco's conclusions correct? Does his classmate dislike him? Is his co-worker a liar? In both cases, no. Neither the classmate nor the colleague was trying to be rude.

The problem in these scenarios was that Marco was unaware of the difference between the speakers' words and their intentions. Marco did not know that "How are you?" "Let's get together," and similar expressions are actually a form of small talk. "How are you?" and "How are you doing?" are not real questions. They are greetings, similar to "Hello." A speaker who uses these expressions does not expect an answer beyond "Fine, thanks."

Likewise, "Let's keep in touch," "I'll call you," or "Let's talk soon" are not invitations or promises to get in touch. They are simply polite ways of closing a conversation.

But if Americans don't mean what they say, how can you know when they are truly interested in knowing about your health or when they're sincerely looking forward to meeting you again? Watch their behavior. If the speaker makes eye contact and waits to hear your answer, chances are they are asking a real question. In the second case, you can recognize a real invitation if the speaker makes an appointment with you for a specific day and time.

The lesson to learn from Marco's experiences is that it isn't always enough to understand the words that people use. You have to know the intention, or purpose, behind them as well.

Page 58, Exercise 2 – CD2 Track 4

Strategies for Successful Small Talk
Opportunities for small talk can happen anywhere: on an airplane, in the school cafeteria, in line for a concert, or before an office meeting. But how do you start a conversation, how do you end it politely, and what should you do in between? Below are tips that will help you fit in just about anywhere.

1. Prepare a list of neutral conversation starters that you can call on in any situation. "Excuse me" is always a good way to get someone's attention before you engage them with a question such as "Do you have the time?", "Where's the bus stop?", or "It's not supposed to rain, is it?"
2. Learn phrases for exiting from conversations gracefully. Useful expressions include "It's been great talking to you, but I really have to go," "It was nice talking to you," or "Excuse

me, I have to . . ." As you are walking away, you can add "Take care," "See you later," or "Take it easy."
3. Work on your listening skills and practice making listening sounds. "I see," "Yes, of course," "Uh-huh," "Really," or "Wow!" show you are listening and focused on what the other person is saying.
4. Use positive body language. Use a mirror to practice smiling, making eye contact, and nodding. Americans will interpret these behaviors as signals that you are paying attention.
5. Learn how to interrupt politely. Say "Excuse me," "Pardon me," or "Sorry," and then follow up with a question about what the speaker has just said. In American culture, it is not always rude to cut in when another person is speaking; on the contrary, interrupting sometimes shows that you are actively involved in the conversation.
6. Write down funny stories you hear or interesting experiences you've had. Then practice saying them aloud. Telling a funny story is an excellent way to break the ice.
7. Most of all, don't be shy! In the United States, it is normal to start up a casual conversation with someone you've never met before. So the next time you're standing in line at the supermarket, don't be afraid to say to the person in front of you, "Nice day, isn't it?"

Unit 7

Page 63, Exercises 2A and 2B – CD2 Track 5

The topic of my talk today is teamwork. If you've ever had a job interview, chances are that the interviewer asked you what teamwork means to you, or whether you're a team player, right? Well, what is teamwork, and why is it important?
Let's start with a definition: Teamwork means working together as a group, or team. A long time ago, we only used this word to talk about sports, like a baseball team, but these days it means any group of people who collaborate, I mean, who work and think together, to accomplish a common goal. Just a few examples are a team of workers working to find a way to reduce their company's use of electricity, or a group of students working together to design a park, or a group of volunteers who are working on a plan to raise money for their children's school.
Teamwork is important because it makes it easier to accomplish goals. Especially

when you have a large project, it's easier and faster to complete the task when you have a team of people with different strengths and abilities working on different pieces of it. So teamwork benefits organizations, but it can also benefit individuals. If you work as a team at your job or school, you will feel more invested in what you are doing because other people on your team are depending on you.
Teamwork has other important benefits, too. According to research, organizations that use teamwork have better employee and student involvement and reduced absenteeism – fewer people missing work or school because of stress or illness. Additionally, when people work together in a group, they learn valuable skills such as conflict resolution and how to come to a consensus, or agreement. And workers or students involved in teamwork are more adaptable and flexible because they learn to work with people who have different work and study habits and styles.
For these reasons, teamwork is an essential part of today's society, in both the workplace and in academic settings. Traditionally, American society has encouraged individuals to act independently in order to rise up in the world, but these days more and more organizations are recognizing the value of people working together to reach common goals.

Page 66, Exercise 2 – CD2 Track 6

Bad Behavior in the Workplace
A recent survey by Randstad USA, an employer staffing firm, asked over 1,500 U.S. employees to identify the things co-workers do that they find most annoying. Number one on the list of the seven worst behaviors was gossiping, the passing around of rumors and intimate information.
Other employee pet peeves included wasting company time with poor time-management skills, colleagues who leave messes in common areas such as the lunch or meeting rooms, unpleasant scents and loud noises in the office, overuse of phones and laptops in meetings, and misuse of company email (for example, emailing too often or copying too many people on messages).
But the list of bothersome behaviors in the workplace did not end there. It included abusive behaviors like bullying and sexual harassment. An earlier survey done by the online learning provider SkillSoft found bullying by co-workers and management to be a top employee concern.

"Bullying" is defined as behavior done by a person with greater power for the purpose of intimidating, or frightening, a weaker or less powerful person. The term "bully" is usually associated with a child who behaves badly, but a manager who repeatedly criticizes a worker in front of co-workers, or a professor who ridicules a student's religious beliefs or appearance, may also be guilty of bullying.

Sexual harassment – which includes inappropriate touching or sexual remarks and using threats to force unwanted sexual activity on an employee or fellow student – is a serious workplace abuse. Both males and females can be targets of sexual harassment.

Both bullying and sexual harassment are against the law. All government and state offices, as well as colleges, have written policies that define and prohibit these behaviors. So do most large companies. The U.S. Equal Employment Opportunity Commission, or EEOC, is the government agency in charge of enforcing laws against discrimination, which includes sexual harassment.

Annoying colleagues, bad work etiquette, and abusive behavior can all lead to unhappy working conditions that affect worker productivity and satisfaction. Well-managed organizations have rules and procedures in place to define improper behavior and prevent these abuses.

Page 68, Exercise 2 – CD2 Track 7

Don't Let Annoying People Drive You Nuts
How many times have you had to put up with a phone ringing in someone's pocket in class, the loud talker in the seat behind you on a plane, or the choking smell of perfume in the office meeting room? When someone's behavior annoys you, what do you do? Well, if you don't know the offending person or aren't tied to the situation, you can get up and leave. But what if you can't leave, or if you're forced to share space with a person who regularly drives you up a wall – what then?

Getting Angry Isn't the Answer
Experts in group relations say that getting angry with an annoying person only makes a bad situation worse. A confrontation can put you in a bad mood, increase your stress level, and make you say things that you might regret later. However, turning a blind eye to the problem and doing nothing will only make you more resentful, and it won't make things better.

The Direct Approach Is Often the Best
If you decide the problem is bad enough, and if you can't avoid it by changing office desks or moving to a different part of the classroom, many experts agree that addressing the problem head-on is your best approach. But be careful. If you sound overly critical or accusatory, your attempt to clear the air might backfire and make matters worse.

Instead of criticizing, experts suggest a more constructive approach. First, try to take into account the other person's feelings. He or she may not be aware of their annoying behavior. Just letting the person know your point of view – without criticizing or putting blame on them – is a healthy approach. Use "I" language instead of "you" language. For example, saying "I would appreciate you keeping your voice down a little" sounds much less accusatory and mean-spirited than "You talk so loud, I can't hear myself think."

If the annoyance is minor, like a colleague whose gum chewing grates on your nerves, don't make a big deal out of it. An indirect or joking comment may be sufficient: "Hey, I guess that gum tastes really good! But I'm having trouble concentrating – could you please chew more quietly?"

In short, when it comes to dealing with annoying classmates or co-workers, a little diplomacy goes a long way.

Unit 8

Page 73, Exercises 2A and 2B – CD2 Track 8

No one likes to receive criticism, right? And I'm sure all of us have been in situations where a boss or a teacher or a parent criticized us and we didn't respond well to the criticism. But just as important as knowing how to handle criticism is knowing how to give criticism that's fair and constructive, and that's the topic of my lecture today.

Let's look at the case of a student named Ray who was criticized by his professor. Last week Ray had an important exam. He studied as much as he could, but it wasn't enough, because when he got his exam back the first thing he saw was a big red F at the top of his paper. The professor had circled all the wrong answers in red and had written "Disappointing performance – See me in my office" at the bottom of the paper.

The professor didn't know that Ray is extremely busy because, in addition to his course load, he also works part-time.

He usually has to stay up late at night to get his homework done, and lots of times he goes to bed at 2:00 a.m. after getting home from his restaurant job at 11:00 p.m. Ray went to see his professor and tried to explain his situation, but the professor wasn't sympathetic. "You need to try harder," he said. "If you can't handle working and studying at the same time, maybe you should think about quitting school."

This made Ray so angry that he slammed the door on the way out of his professor's office. But then he started to think that maybe his professor was right. And three weeks later, he dropped out of school. Now, what can we learn from this scenario? We see that negative criticism can have terrible consequences. It can make people angry and cause them to lose confidence and motivation.

If you have to criticize someone, experts say, do it constructively, or positively. Constructive criticism has three steps: First, say something good about the person or their work. This will help them relax and prepare them for the next step. In step two, talk to the person about their mistakes. Be honest, but be gentle. And don't stop there – talk to the person about solutions to the problem. The goal is to help a person learn and grow, not to hurt or embarrass them. Finally, in the third step, offer another positive statement about the person that lets them know you care about them. This will leave the person feeling motivated instead of discouraged. Imagine if Ray's professor had followed these steps. He might have been able to help Ray instead of causing him to drop out of school.

Page 76, Exercise 2 – CD2 Track 9

Accepting Criticism Gracefully
Accepting criticism gracefully is not an easy thing to do. Criticism can be extremely hurtful and can make us feel exposed and vulnerable. In her article "Handling Criticism with Honesty and Grace," communications expert Kare Anderson offers some insights into why criticism makes us feel so bad and how to lessen the pain.

Anderson states that criticism is so powerful because when we receive it, we are like animals under attack. "Your heart beats faster [and] your skin temperature goes down . . . your instincts are to focus on that feeling," which makes it stronger. Criticism, she adds, makes people want to either run away or fight back.

Anderson says it is important to focus on the content of the critical comments and not to let defensive emotions build up inside us. Putting up defenses may lead us to take "a superior or righteous position, get more rigid, and listen less as the criticism continues."

Anderson encourages people to follow a four-step process when responding to criticism.

1. Step one is to show, either verbally or with a simple nod, that you heard the criticism. Staying calm and saying something like "I understand how 1 concerned you are about this" is much better than saying "You are totally wrong" or "You don't know what you are talking about."

2. Step two is to ask for more information, even if you disagree with the criticism. This will help both parties understand the message. Anderson says, "The more fully the [critical] person feels heard, the more likely he or she will be receptive to your response."

3. In step three, both parties should seek to find something they can agree on in the message. Usually there is some kernel of truth in criticism. Take responsibility for at least that much. If there is nothing at all to agree upon, however, look at the positive intentions of the critical party, saying something like "I understand your need to be very thorough." or "If I had known how much you cared about the project, . . ."

4. Step four is responding to the criticism, but always after asking permission first. If you disagree with the criticism, you can say, "May I give you my opinion?" or "What can we do to make things better?" However, Anderson says, "if [on the other hand] you believe the [critical] comments are accurate, say so. If an apology is in order, give it sooner rather than later."

Page 78, Exercise 2 – CD2 Track 10

The Performance Evaluation

Serena was sitting in the office cafeteria reading the newspaper when her friend John walked in. He looked rather sad. John poured himself a cup of coffee and walked over to her. "Hi," he said, slumping down into a chair.

Serena looked up from her paper. "Looks like things didn't go well with your evaluation," she said.

"Nope, it was awful."

"What happened?" she asked.

"I messed up," said John. "I lost my cool when Bill said some things about my performance I didn't agree with."

"Why did you do that?" asked Serena.

"I don't know really. I felt hurt, I guess, and embarrassed."

Serena put down her paper. "What exactly did he say?"

"Well, first," said John, "he said I need to use my time better, you know, stop chitchatting so much with co-workers because I wasn't working fast enough." John looked up at her. "Just hearing it started my heart racing and all I could think about was how bad it made me feel. Then he said a few more negative things."

"What more did he say?"

"You know," answered John, "I'm not really sure. I can't remember now."

"You can't remember . . . weren't you listening?" asked Serena.

"Well, yes and no . . . you see, I started to get all defensive and started talking about what a good job I do and how much I disagreed with him." John shook his head. "Then I started blabbing about my workload and how the other folks in my department aren't pulling their weight."

"You started blaming others?" said Serena.

"Yeah, I know," John said, looking over at her. "Bad, huh?" He drank his coffee and stared into his cup. "I was so surprised and embarrassed, I just blew up."

John thought for a moment, then said, "I wish I could do it over again. If I had known he was so displeased with my work, I would have been more prepared for the criticism. Maybe I would have been more calm."

John suddenly stood up.

"Where are you going?" asked Serena.

"First I'm going to email Bill an apology and ask for another meeting," he said, sliding his chair beneath the table, "and then I'm getting back to work."

Unit 9

Page 83, Exercises 2A and 2B – CD2 Track 11

Welcome, everyone, to today's workshop, which we're calling "Adjusting Your Attitude for Success." As everybody knows, attitude affects all aspects of our lives – the people around us, the success of our work, and the enjoyment of our daily tasks. Whether you think you have a positive or a negative attitude, this class will help you to become more successful at work, at school, and at home. OK?

To begin, how do you recognize a positive person? Well, behavior can reveal a lot about a person's attitude. Positive people are generally upbeat and cheerful. They smile a lot, even if they're stressed out. They're usually inspired by their work and try to do their best. They have a "can-do" attitude, meaning they welcome challenges and believe that there's a solution to every problem. Positive people also support their teammates or co-workers. They like to shine a light on other people's accomplishments, and they rarely complain. In short, positive people are a pleasure to be around.

Now let's look at the opposite type of person, the person nobody wants to have on their team because of their negative attitude. How do they behave? Well, typically, negative people don't smile or laugh very much, and they always seem to be unhappy about something. They are often critical or sarcastic, and they tend to be much more focused on themselves than on others. They complain that no one wants to eat lunch with them, but they can't see that it's their own negativity that is pushing friends, family, and colleagues away. Do you know anybody like that?

Now these are extreme descriptions, of course. Nobody is totally positive or totally negative all the time. But if you feel there's too much negativity in your life and you'd like to take steps to fix it, this class will give you the skills you need to adjust your attitude for a better and more successful life. So let's get started.

Page 86, Exercise 2 – CD2 Track 12

The Power of Positive Thinking

Hugo Abitbol came to the United States from Morocco 12 years ago. He went to college, found a job, got married, and had a son. His life was happy and normal in every way – until one day five years ago, when his idyllic world was turned upside down. On that day, Hugo learned he had invasive prostate cancer. Although he was still a young man, he needed immediate surgery to save his life. He had the operation and spent two months recovering. Now, five years later, he is working and enjoying life as much as ever, even though he knows that the cancer could return any time.

"When life gives you a setback, you can't surrender. You can't give up. You have to persevere, although it's not always easy to keep going," Hugo said.

Hugo is sure it was his positive attitude that helped him overcome the cancer. It wasn't easy. At first, his family was stunned and upset. Hugo told them that they would deal with the challenges of his illness one day at a time.

"You can't stop living just because you have problems," Hugo said. "Even though life can be discouraging, you need to keep moving forward."

Following his surgery, Hugo took several positive steps to speed up his recovery. He joined a support group for cancer survivors. Connecting with other people reminded him that he was not alone and helped him deal with his anxiety about the future.

Also, he was determined to get back to his job managing a garden supply business. Hugo had always adored plants, and he enjoyed interacting with the customers. Having a job he loved helped him stay focused throughout his recovery.

Today, in addition to his job, Hugo volunteers with charities around Miami to help raise awareness about cancer. "I believe if you have the right attitude," he said, "positive things will happen. I count my blessings every day. I know I'm lucky to be here."

Page 88, Exercise 2 – CD2 Track 13

Say No to Negativitis
Meet Nelly. Even though she is healthy, does well in her night-school classes, and has a good job, Nelly finds something to complain about in almost every situation. It's a beautiful spring day? "All those flowers make me sneeze." She gets an A minus on a difficult homework assignment? "I should have gotten an A." She gets a pay increase at work? "It's only $20 a week. Big deal."

We all know people like Nelly. Critical, unsmiling, and gloomy, such people seem to have a disease that prevents them from seeing the bright side of life. Some psychologists even have a name for their negative attitude – "negativitis."

The causes of negativitis can be complex. Some people have a negative attitude because of difficulties in their childhood or personal lives. In other people, negativity is a response to unfair treatment. At work, for example, negativitis can develop from employees feeling that they are underpaid or overworked, that their successes are not recognized, or that they are not included in decision making.

Just one person's negative attitude can be enough to contaminate the atmosphere of an entire office or group. Workplaces infected with negativitis show increases in absenteeism, accidents, employee mistakes, and theft. Unless managers recognize employee negativity and take steps to eradicate it, it can lead to major financial losses.

Although management should take an active role in solving the problem of workplace negativity, you, as an employee, can also take steps to combat the toxic effects of negativitis in your workplace or group:

1. Whenever possible, avoid negative, complaining co-workers.
2. Control your own negative comments and negative thinking. Choose to think and speak positively.
3. Don't participate in office gossip.
4. Make a list of all the negative words you hear other people using. Remove those words from your vocabulary.
5. Notice and acknowledge other people's good work. Be generous with compliments.
6. Keep the lines of communication open with your boss and co-workers. Seek positive solutions to problems.

Unit 10

Page 93, Exercises 2A and 2B – CD2 Track 14

OK, today I want to talk to you about the importance of writing. No matter what your future job is, chances are you will have to do some kind of writing. For example, nursing assistants have to write daily progress reports on their patients. Automotive technicians need to write work orders for cars that need repairs. Housekeepers have to write shopping lists. To show just how important writing is, let me quote you some of the findings from a 2010 report by the National Commission on Writing for America's Families, Schools, and Colleges.

Number one: Two-thirds, that's more than 60 percent, of salaried workers in large American companies – that means full-time, career workers – have to do some kind of writing in their jobs.
Number two: Among hourly workers, between 20 and 35 percent of workers also have some writing responsibility.
Number three: Moving into the future, job seekers who cannot write well will probably not get hired, and workers who already have jobs may not get promoted if they don't have good writing skills.
Number four: Good writing skills are so important that the Commission found that companies spend up to three billion dollars a year on improving their workers' writing skills to make them more productive.
The Commission's conclusion was that in today's job market, writing skills are just as important as math and computer skills. Furthermore, if you learn to write well in school, it will transfer to almost any job, from taking orders in a restaurant to writing business reports for a company. But if you don't learn how to write well, you could end up with a low-paying job and have no options for promotion.

So if you want to improve your writing skills, take classes and practice writing as much as possible. And have patience. It takes time to learn how to write well, but if you practice regularly, you can learn how to write more clearly, accurately, and concisely.

Page 96, Exercise 2 – CD2 Track 15

Email Etiquette 101
The use of electronic communication has exploded throughout the world in the last decade. In the United States, recent studies have shown that 92 percent of all Internet users communicate via email. Innovative forms of electronic communication, such as text messaging and "tweeting" (sending short messages of less than 140 characters), are becoming more popular among teens and other computer-savvy people. However, most electronic communication at work and at school still revolves around email messages.

Unfortunately, while many classes and seminars focus on correct ways to write a report or business letter, few, if any, stress the importance of using proper email etiquette. To avoid miscommunication and angry responses, follow these rules:

Composing email
Be sure to clearly say what the message is about in the subject line. If the subject in your subject line is too vague, your email may not even be read.
With bosses, instructors, and new business contacts, keep email formal until you are told that using first names is OK. Keep your email brief and make the tone friendly and respectful. Remember to use good manners, like saying "please" and "thank you."
Don't type in all capital or in all lowercase letters. The first way may make it look like you are shouting, and the second may suggest that you are lazy.
Remember that email messages are not private and that they can be seen by other people. Never fight or gossip in an email message at work.

Sending and forwarding email
Wait to enter the address until after you write the email. That way, you will be more likely to complete the message before sending it. Take time to proofread both the

message and the address. Refrain from using the "Reply all" feature unless you are sure everyone on the list needs to read it.

Responding to email in a timely manner is essential. Even if you can't reply right away, send a response saying you received the message and will respond more fully later. If you want to send a large attachment with an email, ask first. If an attachment is too large, it may not be delivered. It may be best to break up a large attachment into a few smaller ones and to attach them to several different emails.

When it comes to forwarding email, always add a comment to the forwarded message to tell why you are forwarding it and to identify yourself. And remember, do not send personal email from your workplace.

Page 98, Exercise 2 – CD2 Track 16

Good Business Writing Doesn't Beat Around the Bush

The daily workplace is filled with writing of all sorts, lengths, and purposes, generated by both workers and management. Emails, letters, memos, and reports are regularly distributed and read to keep information flowing smoothly.

The workplace is also filled with lots to read from the outside world. Newspapers, journals, news releases, and documents of all kinds are required reading for businesspeople who want to stay informed and on top of new developments.

But because time is short, businesspeople often just skim or only partially read things in order to extract the information they need. Therefore, it's key for business writing to be clear, crisp, and to the point. All forms of effective writing in the workplace share several common qualities:

The K.I.S.S. Technique

First and foremost, good business writing uses the K.I.S.S. technique, meaning Keep It Short and Simple. The idea is to convey information in simple, well-organized, and easy-to-read terms. You can avoid confusion by using short sentences when possible and keeping the language simple and familiar. This aids the comprehension of readers who may not have time to read the material in depth.

Directness

Good business writing doesn't beat around the bush, but instead is direct, specific, and to the point. Fuzzy, abstract phrases, such as "a nice person" or "a good idea," force readers to slow down and guess at their real meaning. Concrete, descriptive phrases, such as "a generous young woman" or "an innovative suggestion," enable readers to form clearer images in their minds.

The Active Voice

The passive voice can sometimes confuse readers because it does not say who the performer of an action is. In business writing, it is especially important to be clear about exactly who is doing what. Thus, instead of saying "Arrangements were made to ship your order immediately," you can write "I made arrangements to ship your order immediately." Instead of "Your complaint is being investigated," write "I am having my assistant investigate your complaint." The active voice not only tells the reader who is responsible for performing the action, it is also more interesting and attention grabbing.

ACKNOWLEDGMENTS

The authors and publishers acknowledge the following sources of copyright material and are grateful for the permissions granted. While every effort has been made, it has not always been possible to identify the sources of all the material used, or to trace all copyright holders. If any omissions are brought to our notice, we will be happy to include the appropriate acknowledgments on reprinting and in the next update to the digital edition, as applicable.

Key: B = Below, L = Left, R = Right, T = Top.

Photos

All images are sourced from Getty Images.

p. 2 (photo 1): Steve Debenport/E+; p. 2 (photo 2, photo 4), p. 62 (photo 2), p. 85 (L): Hero Images; p. 2 (photo 3): Jacob Wackerhausen/E+; p. 12 (T): Jose Luis Pelaez Inc/Blend Images; p. 12 (B): Thomas Barwick/DigitalVision; p. 21: PhotoAlto/Sigrid Olsson/PhotoAlto Agency RF Collections; p. 22 (photo 1): Rebecca Emery/DigitalVision; p. 22 (photo 2): Hill Street Studios/Blend Images; p. 22 (photo 3): Klaus Vedfelt/DigitalVision; p. 32 (photo 1): YinYang/E+; p. 32 (photo 2): AndreyPopov/iStock/Getty Images Plus; p. 32 (photo 3): Ariel Skelley/DigitalVision; p. 32 (photo 4): UltraONEs/iStock/Getty Images Plus; p. 42 (photo 1): Dave and Les Jacobs/Blend Images; p. 42 (photo 2): sturti/iStock/Getty Images Plus; p. 42 (photo 3), p. 72 (photo 4): shironosov/iStock/Getty Images Plus; p. 42 (photo 4): Klaus Vedfelt/Taxi; p. 52 (photo 1): Paul Bradbury/OJO Images; p. 52 (photo 2): Portra/DigitalVision; p. 52 (photo 3): Reza Estakhrian/Photolibrary; p. 52 (photo 4): Will Woods/Photodisc; p. 62 (photo 1): Blend Images - LWA/Dann Tardif/ Brand X Pictures; p. 62 (photo 3), p. 92 (photo 5): PeopleImages/DigitalVision; p. 62 (photo 4): Chris Ryan/OJO Images; p. 65: Rob Lewine; p. 72 (photo 1): Ezra Bailey/Taxi; p. 72 (photo 2): PhotoAlto/Eric Audras/PhotoAlto Agency RF Collections; p. 72 (photo 3): Viktorcvetkovic/iStock/Getty Images Plus; p. 75: RADsan/iStock/Getty Images Plus; p. 82 (photo 1): David Lees/DigitalVision; p. 82 (photo 2): Prasit photo/Moment; p. 82 (photo 3): Sam Edwards/Caiaimage; p. 82 (photo 4): Gpointstudio/Image Source; p. 85 (R): DigitalVision; p. 92 (photo 1): Blend Images - ERproductions Ltd/Brand X Pictures; p. 92 (photo 2): kupicoo/E+; p. 92 (photo 3): Jupiterimages/Stockbyte; p. 92 (photo 4): Cultura RM Exclusive/Matelly/Cultura Exclusive.

Front Cover Photography by RichVintage/E+/Getty Images.

Back Cover Photography by pressureUA/iStock/Getty Images Plus; Adidet Chaiwattanakul/EyeEm; pixelfit/E+.

Audio produced by CityVox.